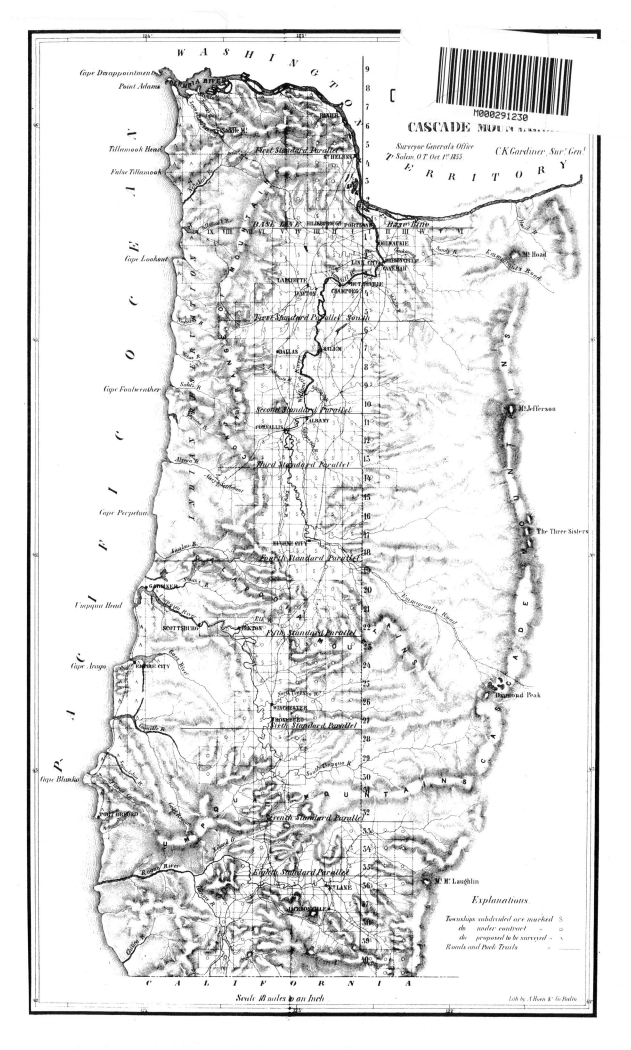

**OREGON COAST
AQUARIUM**

Seafood Cookbook

Leslie J. Whipple Mansfield

— A Maverick Publication —

ISBN 0-89288-262-X

Library of Congress Catalog Card Number: 96-78146

CREDITS

Cover Photo Design and Food Styling—Leslie J. Whipple-Mansfield

Cover Photography—Gene Balcomb and Elizabeth Lawhead Bourne

Layout and Design—Bridget R. Wise

To order additional copies, contact:

Maverick Distributors
Drawer 7289
Bend, Oregon 97708

(541) 382-2728
1-800-333-8046

Published and printed by
Maverick Publications
P.O. Box 5007
Bend, Oregon 97708

*For my husband
Richard,
with love and deep appreciation.*

Acknowledgments

I wish to thank:

Richard Mansfield

Stewart M. Whipple

Marcia J. Whipple

Doran L. Whipple

Michelle Marquart

Phyllis Bell

Nyna Somerville

Carrie Meidell

Elizabeth Lawhead Bourne

Gene Balcomb

Gary Asher

Bridget Wise

H. Bruce Miller

This book would not have been possible without the contributions and cooperation of many people: chefs, restaurants, wineries, and especially the staff and friends of the Oregon Coast Aquarium, who made their recipes, stories and expertise available to *The Oregon Coast Aquarium Seafood Cookbook*. I wish to thank them all for their generosity.

Table of Contents

Appetizers & Salads 15

Soups & Stews 29

Pasta & Rice 47

Salmon 67

Seafood 91

Shellfish 119

Restaurant Index 131

Index 133

Mission Statement

The Oregon Coast Aquarium is a financially self-supporting, non-profit, public aquatic and marine science exhibition facility of the highest quality dedicated to public enjoyment, education and research so the public will better understand and cherish the natural resources of the Oregon Coast.

OREGON COAST
AQUARIUM

Introduction

From the minute Leslie Whipple-Mansfield first approached me about putting together this cookbook, I knew we had a project after my own heart. I come from a large, loud, food-loving family that marks every major holiday, milestone and get-together with lavish meals. When I was a girl, my grandmother taught me the art of preparing Italian delicacies like homemade raviolis, linguini with clam sauce and ricotta pies—dishes I still look forward to fixing when time and a good rainy day permit. From the Slovenian side of my family I learned the magic of polenta and cioppino. Each December I still set aside entire baking days for the pizelles, kourbiedes and biscotti that my friends, colleagues and family count on receiving each year. The very smell of homemade bread sets me on a straight and unbroken path to my earliest memories of childhood.

What contribution can be richer, more saturated with personal meaning, than a recipe, containing weights, measures, ingredients and instructions, but also inseparable memory? The well-loved recipes you will find in these pages were contributed by the Oregon Coast Aquarium's friends, board of directors, volunteers and staff. On behalf of all of us, I hope you enjoy preparing and eating these as much as we've enjoyed developing, testing, tasting, and including them here.

Phyllis Bell, President
Oregon Coast Aquarium

Sandy Shores Stories

Sea stars run on water power

Pink sea stars, indeed all sea stars, have hundreds of tiny feet lining the grooves on their bellies. These flexible, hollow "tube feet" have suction-cup tips to help stars walk over slippery rocks and pull open shellfish to eat.

A sea star pumps seawater in and out of its tube feet to extend and retract them. Somehow all those feet manage to work together, pushing and pulling the star along, turning it any which way but loose.

Where does beach sand come from?

Beach sand is a combination of crushed shells and tiny grains of rock. Some new grains come from eroding coastal cliffs and some are carried by rivers that empty into the sea. But on Oregon's beaches, much of the sand has been there for thousands of years.

Invertebrate (in VUR tuh brayt)
Vertebrate (VUR tuh brayt)

Scientists classify animals into two main categories: those with backbones and those without. Animals with backbones, called vertebrates, include fishes, birds and mammals: Complex animals with internal skeletons supported by a backbone.

Invertebrates are hard to describe as a group because the only trait they all share is their lack of a spine. More than 95 percent of all animals are invertebrates: shrimps, sponges, squids, sea anemones, sea stars, sea pens, clams, crabs, corals, chitons, jellyfishes, octopuses, barnacles, limpets, mussels, abalones, amphipods . . .

Crustacean (kruhs TAY shuhn)

Crustaceans have jointed legs, gills for breathing and a hard shell called an exoskeleton. The name crustacean refers to the crusty texture of their exoskeleton which the animals must shed periodically in order to grow.

Crustaceans, which are related to spiders and insects, include crabs, lobsters, beach hoppers, shrimps and barnacles. Crustaceans also make up a large part of the zooplankton, tiny animals that drift with ocean currents.

Crabs aren't picky about their food

Some use their pincers to chip open the shells of clams, oysters and barnacles. Others clip algae from the rocks and use their spoon-shaped claws to carry food to their mouths.

You aren't the only one fond of crab. Many fishes and shorebirds eat adults crabs. Salmon and other open ocean fishes feed on the young drifting larvae. Crabs cope with their popularity as a menu item by producing 700,000 or more young per crab each year.

Sand gets in their claws

The Dungeness crab, and other crabs that live on the sandy seafloor, have lightweight shells and nimble legs. They scurry lightly over the sand on the tips of their legs in the familiar sideways crabwalk.

Some of these crabs burrow backward into the seafloor when danger appears. Special bristles keep sand grains out of their gills while the crabs are hiding. Only their eyes and antennae peek out, watching till the threat passes by.

Sandy Shores

OREGON COAST AQUARIUM

"The shore is an ancient world. For as long as there has been an earth and sea there has been this place of meeting of land and water."

Rachel Carson

Highlights of this gallery include a free-standing Piers and Pilings exhibit. The 4,730-gallon tank replicates the unique habitat formed by man-made docks and piers. A cross-section of a wave-lapped sandy beach shows what animals live in the sand. In all, the gallery holds 13 separate exhibits.

Animals exhibited in the Sandy Shores include leopard sharks, flatfishes, beach hoppers, skates, sea pens, sand dollars and surf perch.

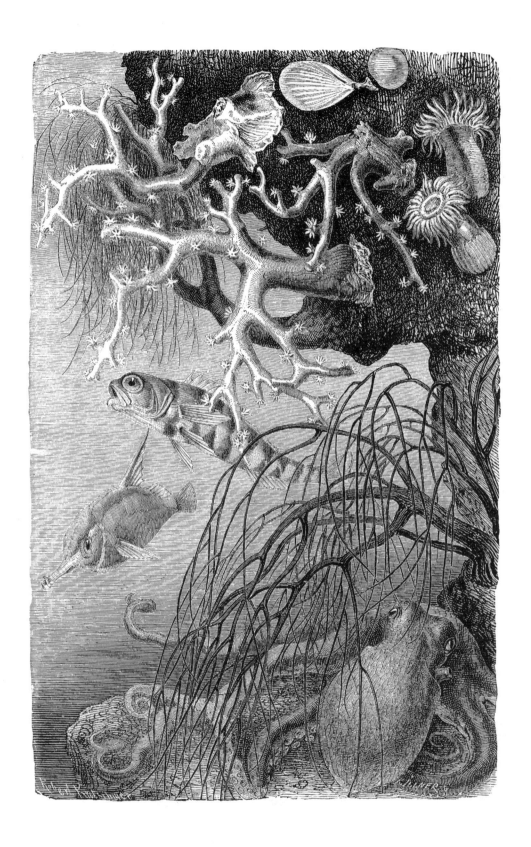

Appetizers
and
Salads

**OREGON COAST
AQUARIUM**

Cozze Ripini
(Stuffed Mussels on the Half Shell)

36 mussels, scrubbed and debearded
1/4 cup minced parsley
2 cloves garlic, minced
1 tablespoon olive oil

1/4 teaspoon lemon juice
1/4 teaspoon pepper
1/2 cup Italian seasoned dry
    bread crumbs

Preheat oven to 350 degrees.

In a large pot, add enough water to come 1-inch up the sides of the pot. Bring to a boil over high heat. Add mussels, cover tightly, and steam about 5 to 7 minutes or until mussels open. Discard any unopened mussels. Remove from heat and remove mussels with a slotted spoon. Remove 2 tablespoons of cooking liquid and set aside. Break shells apart and discard the top half. Replace mussels that have been dislodged while steaming. Place mussels on the half shell on baking sheets and set aside.

In a small bowl, combine reserved 2 tablespoons mussel cooking liquid, parsley, garlic, olive oil, lemon juice and pepper and blend well. Place a dab on each mussel. Sprinkle bread crumbs on top. Bake until top is nicely browned. Serves 6.

Chris Pontrelli and Jim Burley

Crabs

Crabs molt as they grow, splitting their shells at the seams and then crawling out in a brand new suit. When you see an empty shell, chances are the crab's not dead, but alive and well, one size larger down the beach.

Hot Crab Dip

1 (8-ounce) package cream cheese
1/4 cup mayonnaise
1 tablespoon minced onion
1 teaspoon Dijon mustard
1 teaspoon sugar

1 clove garlic, minced
1/4 teaspoon salt
1 cup crabmeat
3 tablespoons dry white wine

In the top of a double-boiler, melt the cream cheese. Stir in the mayonnaise, onion, mustard, sugar, garlic and salt and simmer together for 5 minutes. Stir in crabmeat and wine and heat through. Serve with French bread.

Patty Martin

Smoked Salmon Log

1 pound cooked salmon OR
    1 (16-ounce) can red salmon,
    bones and skin removed
1 (8-ounce) package cream cheese, at room
    temperature
1 tablespoon lemon juice
1 tablespoon grated onion

1 teaspoon horseradish
1 teaspoon liquid smoke flavoring
1/4 teaspoon salt
1/8 teaspoon Tabasco sauce
1 cup chopped pecans
1 tablespoon minced parsley

In a large bowl, combine salmon, cream cheese, lemon juice, onion, horseradish, liquid smoke, salt and Tabasco and mix until smooth. Chill and form into a log. Combine pecans and parsley on a plate and roll log to coat evenly. Chill until ready to serve. Serve with crackers.

Patty Martin

Smoky Salmon Spread

1 (7-3/4-ounce) can Alaskan sockeye salmon
1 (8-ounce) package cream cheese, softened
3 tablespoons sliced green onions

3 drops liquid smoke flavoring
Crackers or toasted bagels

Drain and flake salmon reserving 2 teaspoons of liquid. Place salmon and reserved liquid in a large bowl. Add cream cheese, green onions and liquid smoke flavoring and blend well. Cover and refrigerate at least 2 hours or overnight to allow flavors to marry. Serve with crackers or toasted bagels. Makes about 1-1/2 cups.

Alan and Alice Beardsley

Clam and Cheese Dip

1 (8-ounce) package cream cheese
1 (6-ounce) can chopped clams, reserve juice
1 medium onion, finely chopped
2 tablespoons cottage cheese
2 tablespoons mayonnaise

1/2 teaspoon lemon juice
1/4 teaspoon Tabasco sauce
1/4 teaspoon Worcestershire sauce
Salt and pepper to taste

In a medium bowl, blend cream cheese with reserved clam juice until smooth. Add remaining ingredients and mix until well blended. Chill for at least 3 hours to allow flavors to marry. Serve with crackers or crudité.

Patty Martin

 ## Smoked Salmon Paté

2 (4-ounce) packages of Siletz Tribal
    Smokehouse Smoked Salmon, flaked
1 (8-ounce) package cream cheese
1/2 cup chopped black olives

1/2 teaspoon garlic powder
Sesame seeds OR chopped walnuts for
    garnish

Cream together salmon (including juices), cream cheese and garlic powder. Add olives and mix well. Shape into a ball or log. Roll in sesame seeds or chopped walnuts. Serve with crackers or crudité.

LaRita Lundy
Siletz Tribal Smokehouse

Building a Beach

The life of a beach

    Restless waves wash up the beach, churning the sand and everything in it. Winds and high tides drive seawater toward the dunes. Wide expanses of beach are exposed to drying air at low tide and are flooded again when the tide rises.

    The power of the sea shapes the coast. Beaches change daily and hourly, responding to the waves, winds, currents and tides. Jetties and other man-made structures come and go, but in the end, the sea is in control.

As the tides turn

    The gravitational pulls of the moon and sun create a bulge of water in the ocean. Centrifugal force from the earth's spin creates another bulge on the opposite side of the planet. The bulges form high tides and the low water between bulges forms low tides.

    Spring tides, with the highest high and lowest low tides, occur when the moon and sun line up to combine their pulls. Neap tides, with the lowest high and highest low tides, occur when the moon and sun are at right angles and work against each other's gravity.

 ## Crab Salad

1 head cauliflower
1 large bunch broccoli
2 pounds crab meat
1/2 red onion, diced

1 cup purchased coleslaw dressing
1 cup sour cream
1 teaspoon black pepper

Cut cauliflower and broccoli into bite-sized pieces using only the tops. Reserve the stalks for another use. Place cauliflower florets, broccoli florets, crab meat, onion, coleslaw dressing, sour cream, and pepper in a large bowl and toss well. Refrigerate 2 hours before serving to allow flavors to marry. Serves 8 to 10.

Char Drobney
The Sea Basket

 ## Seafood Slaw

1 cup mayonnaise
3 tablespoons cider vinegar
2 tablespoons sugar
1 teaspoon onion powder
Salt and pepper to taste

1 small head green cabbage, finely chopped
1 large carrot, grated
2 stalks celery, chopped
8 ounces bay shrimp OR crab meat

In a large bowl, combine mayonnaise, vinegar, sugar, onion powder, salt, and pepper and blend well. Add cabbage, carrot, celery, and shrimp and toss well. Cover and refrigerate for at least 2 hours to allow flavors to marry. Serve with hot French bread. Serves 4 to 6.

Elaine Stark

Sand dollars are upstanding citizens

Sand dollars live half-buried in sandy areas with a steady current. They tilt themselves up like wheels, broadside to the current. On the flat side, tiny tube feet surrounding the mouth capture food particles sweeping by.

Small, upstanding sand dollars risk getting washed away or knocked flat by large waves. To stabilize themselves, the little animals use sand for ballast, eating the heaviest grains and storing them in their gut. When the sand dollars grow bigger, they spit out the grains.

Mo's® Oyster Night Bean and Shrimp Salad

2 (15-ounce) cans green beans
1 yellow onion, thinly sliced
1 cucumber, thinly sliced
1/2 cup canned sliced mushrooms
1/4 cup chopped pimento

1 cup bay shrimp
1 cup cider vinegar
1/2 cup vegetable oil
1/2 cup water
Salt and pepper to taste

In a large bowl, combine green beans, onion, cucumber, mushrooms, pimento, and shrimp. In a small bowl combine vinegar, oil, water, salt, and pepper and stir well. Pour over bean mixture and toss gently to coat evenly. Cover and refrigerate 2 hours before serving. Serves 4 to 6.

Cindy McEntee
Mo's® Enterprises, Inc.

Asian Dungeness Crab Cakes

Locals from the Oregon Coast look forward to the Dungeness crab season each year.
Asian Dungeness Crab Cakes make an excellent appetizer to accompany almost any meal.

1/2 cup Miracle Whip OR mayonnaise
1/4 cup chopped green onion
1/4 cup chopped waterchestnuts
1 tablespoon soy sauce
1/8 teaspoon dry mustard

Salt and freshly ground white pepper to taste
2 pounds Dungeness crab meat
2 cups fresh breadcrumbs
Vegetable oil

In a large bowl, combine Miracle Whip, green onions, waterchestnuts, soy sauce, mustard, salt, and white pepper. Whisk until well blended. Mix in crab and breadcrumbs. Form into 16 patties of equal size about 3/4-inch thick. Heat a little oil in a large cast iron skillet over medium heat. Cook crab cakes for 3 to 4 minutes on each side, or until golden brown. Serves 16.

Alfred Popp

Tillamook Toast

4 (1-inch thick) slices French bread
Olive oil
4 ounces Dungeness crab meat
1/4 cup mayonnaise

2 tablespoons lemon juice
1 tablespoon Worcestershire sauce
1/8 teaspoon dill
4 slices aged Tillamook Cheddar cheese

Preheat broiler.

Place French bread on a baking sheet and brush with the olive oil. Place under the broiler and toast until very lightly brown.

In a small bowl, combine crab meat, mayonnaise, lemon juice, Worcestershire sauce, and dill. Mix until well blended. Divide onto toasts and top with cheese. Broil until heated through and cheese is melted. Serves 4.

Urbano Salvati, C.E.C.
Chef Instructor
Western Culinary Institute

Hot Crab and Jalapeño Dip

1-1/2 teaspoons olive oil
1/2 medium red bell pepper, seeded and
    chopped
1 (14-ounce) can artichoke hearts, drained
    and chopped
1 cup mayonnaise
1/2 cup freshly grated Parmesan cheese
1/4 cup thinly sliced green onions

1 tablespoon Worcestershire sauce
1 tablespoon minced pickled jalapeño chiles
1-1/2 teaspoons lemon juice
1/2 teaspoon celery salt
Salt and pepper to taste
8 ounces fresh crabmeat
1/3 cup slivered almonds

Preheat oven to 375 degrees. Lightly oil an 8-inch diameter quiche or pie pan with 1-1/2-inch high sides.

In a medium skillet, heat olive oil over medium-high heat. Add bell pepper and sauté until tender. Transfer to a large bowl.

Add artichoke hearts, mayonnaise, Parmesan, green onions, Worcestershire sauce, jalapeño, lemon juice, celery salt, salt, and pepper and stir to combine well. Gently fold in crab meat. Spread mixture evenly in prepared quiche pan. Sprinkle with almonds. Bake until top is light golden brown and mixture is bubbly, about 30 minutes. Serve warm with sliced baguettes.

Ed and Jeanette Hennings

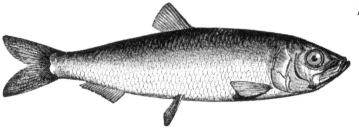

Coconut Beer Battered Prawns

**16 large black tiger prawns (about 1 pound),
    shelled, deveined and butterflied**
Beer Batter (recipe follows)
Shredded coconut
Oil for deep frying
Sticky Sauce (recipe follows)

Dip prawns in beer batter then roll in coconut. Heat oil to 375 degrees and deep fry until golden. Serve with Sticky Sauce. Serves 4.

Beer Batter

1 (12-ounce) bottle beer
1 egg
1/4 teaspoon baking powder
1/4 teaspoon cayenne pepper
1/4 teaspoon celery salt
1/4 teaspoon garlic powder
1/4 teaspoon onion powder
1/4 teaspoon salt
2 cups flour

In a medium bowl, whisk together beer, eggs, baking powder, cayenne pepper, celery salt, garlic powder, onion powder, and salt until smooth. Whisk in flour until a thick batter forms.

Sticky Sauce

8 ounces orange marmalade
2 tablespoons stone ground mustard
2-1/2 teaspoons horseradish

Combine orange marmalade, mustard and horseradish until blended. Allow flavors to marry for 30 minutes before serving.

Peggy O'Dell
Digger O'Dell's Oyster Bar and Restaurant

Oysters

Oysters here by popular demand

Four kinds of oysters grow in Yaquina Bay but the small-size native oysters are the only true locals. They can reproduce in the Bay's chilly water which is too cold for the three imported species. These species—Pacific, suminoi and kumamoto oysters—originally came from Japan. They were brought over to supply the growing consumer market for fresh oysters which has a million-dollar dockside value in Oregon.

How to grow an oyster

Growers purchase oyster larvae from special hatcheries. After settling on empty oyster shells, or clutch, the larvae change form into spat and spend the next two or three years in the bay growing into market-sized adult oysters. The growers scatter spat-covered clutch directly on the mudflats. They also string the clutch on ropes or hang them in net bags and anchor them to rafts in the bay. Individual oysters are raised on tiny pieces of clutch in underwater, mesh-covered trays.

Crab and Artichoke Dip

2 cups finely chopped canned water-packed
artichoke hearts
2 cups fresh crabmeat
2 cups mayonnaise
1/2 cup finely chopped yellow onion

2 teaspoons lemon juice
1 teaspoon freshly ground black pepper
1 teaspoon sea salt
Garnish: Parmesan cheese, minced parsley
and lemon slices

Preheat oven to 425 degrees.

Combine artichoke hearts, crabmeat, mayonnaise, onion, lemon juice, pepper and salt in a medium bowl and mix gently. Spread evenly into an 8-inch by 8-inch oven-proof baking dish and bake until just heated through, about 10 minutes. Garnish with grated Parmesan, parsley and lemon slices. Serve with toasted bread sticks.

Thomas J. Smith, Executive Chef
Oregon Electric Station Restaurant
and Lounge

Taking the best of both worlds

Where the seafloor is soft and sandy, most animals live either over it or in it. Animals over the sand take advantage of food suspended in the water. Animals buried in it find protection and stability.

Safely anchored in the sand, sea pens, burrowing anemones and sand dollars filter fine bits of food from the water. When predators threaten, anemones and sea pens retract into the sand. When storm waves scour the bottom, sand dollars, too, dig in.

Sea pens are a group effort

A sea pen looks and acts like a single organism but it's actually a colony of tiny animals called polyps. Some polyps trap food and some channel water in and out of the colony. Others make slime that glows in the dark.

The lower half of the sea pen, a bulbous foot, is buried in the sandy bottom. when it senses a threat, the sea pen contracts, forcing water out of the colony and retreating into its foot. Once the threat is over, the sea pen comes out to feed again.

Look what the waves dragged in

Just above the high tide mark, beach wrack lies drying in the sun. These tangled heaps of seaweeds and other treasures tossed up by the tide may contain gooseneck barnacles, clam shells, stranded jellyfishes and sometimes even Japanese glass floats.

Constantly removed and replenished by the waves, wrack provides food and shelter for scavengers like kelp flies and beach hoppers. Waves wash nutrients from the decaying seaweeds back to sea to nourish the next crop of algae.

Savory Smoked Salmon and Sausage Pie

2-1/4 cups freshly grated Parmesan cheese
3/4 cups dry bread crumbs
2 tablespoons gumbo file powder
4-1/2 tablespoons butter, melted
8 ounces Italian sausage
8 ounces cream cheese
2 eggs
1 tablespoon Creole seasoning

1 teaspoon black pepper
2/3 cup sour cream
1 tablespoon Pernod OR other
    anise-flavored liquor
2 teaspoons Tabasco sauce
1 teaspoon Worcestershire sauce
8 ounces smoked salmon

Preheat oven to 375 degrees. Oil a 9-inch springform pan and line the bottom with parchment or waxed paper, then oil the parchment.

In a medium bowl, stir together breadcrumbs, 1 cup of the Parmesan cheese, and gumbo file powder until well mixed. Add melted butter and stir until mixture is moistened. Press mixture evenly into prepared springform pan. Bake until golden brown, about 20 minutes. Remove from oven and cool.

Crumble Italian sausage into a large skillet. Cook over medium heat until almost cooked through. Drain well and set aside.

Place cream cheese, eggs, Creole seasoning, and pepper in a mixer with a paddle attachment. Mix well until the cream cheese is smooth and the eggs have been evenly distributed. Add remaining 1-1/4 cups of the Parmesan cheese, sour cream, Pernod, Tabasco sauce, and Worcestershire sauce and mix until well blended. Crumble the smoked salmon into the bowl and add the reserved cooked sausage. Fold in gently but thoroughly.

Reduce oven temperature to 300 degrees. Pour mixture into the prebaked crust. Bake for 45 minutes or until the edges start to look a little dry. Remove from oven and cool completely before serving. Serves 12 as an appetizer.

Larry Lewis, C.E.C, C.C.E.
Executive Chef
Western Culinary Institute

Abalones

An abalone moves at a snail's pace until it meets up with a sea star. Then it spins around, rocks its shell and gallops off with surprising speed. It's no wonder: sea stars enjoy eating fresh abalone as much as people do.

Rocky Shores Stories

What's going on down there?

Life picks up below the low tide line. Dense stands of algae carpet the rocks, thriving in sunlit water. Many kinds of animals live here, exposed to air by only the lowest low tides. Even then they're protected by the lush seaweeds.

Shorter exposure to air means longer exposure to surging water and waves. Attaching themselves to rocks and plants secures the animals from the surge but doesn't protect them from fishes, sea stars and other predators that prowl about below.

Bivalve (BY-valv)

Bivalves are molluscs enclosed in a shell made of two valves. Some live buried in sand or mud, stretching fleshy siphons to the water for food and oxygen. Others have no siphons and swim free, clapping their valves together to move through the water.

Mussels, clams, cockles, oysters and scallops are familiar bivalves. Like most bivalves, they feed by filtering plankton from the water. Shipworms, though, eat wood debris.

Seaweeds support the subtidal zone

The lush algae carpeting the seafloor supports much of the life below the low tide line. Seaweeds can grow as far down as light reaches—100 feet or more in clear seawater. Snails, sea urchins and others graze on the living plants.

Once torn loose by the waves, drifting algae becomes food for scavengers like sea urchins and abalone. Filter-feeders like mussels sift bits of decaying seaweed from the water. Living algae absorb nutrients released by the rotting plants.

Why do so many tidepool animals cling to the rocks?

Tidepool animals must be able to hold on when the tide rises and falls and when waves crash over them. Even below the low tide line, animals need protection because waves reach down as well as up, pushing and pulling animals off the rocks.

Gastropod (GAS tro pawd)

Gastropods are the largest and most varied group of molluscs. Their single broad foot is designed for creeping and clinging to the bottom. Some gastropods are filter-feeders but most have jaws and a rasp-like tongue called a radula which they use to scrape up food. Snails, limpets and abalones are all gastropods. They carry a spiraled shell which they withdraw into or clamp onto rocks for protection. Nudibranchs, or sea slugs, are shell-less gastropods, closely related to the slugs in your garden.

Echinoderm (ee KY no durm)

Echinoderms' spiny skin grows from little calcium plates that form their internal skeletons. Although brainless, echinoderms do have a nervous system. They also possess a unique system of water-filled tubes which they use for moving, eating and even breathing.

Sea stars are typical echinoderms made up of equal parts, usually five, surrounding a central disc like the spokes on a wheel. Sea cucumbers, sea urchins and sand dollars are echinoderms, too, although you have to look at them harder to tell.

Rocky Shores

OREGON COAST
AQUARIUM

*"There is a rapture on the lonely shore,
There is a society where none intrudes,
By the deep sea, with music in its roar."*

Lord Byron

A large touch pool forms the centerpiece of the Rocky Shores Gallery. Staffed at all times, this exhibit lets visitors touch and gently handle tide pool residents, such as sea urchins, sea stars, chitons and anemones. Other gallery highlights include a tidepool cut-away raked by waves, and a deep tidepool in which a visitor-operated videocamera has been mounted, for close-up investigation. The Rocky Shores Gallery holds a total of 15 separate exhibits.

Animals exhibited in the Rocky Shore Gallery include Pacific spiny lumpsuckers, wolf eels, sculpins, decorated warbonnet and a wide range of sea stars, anemones and other animals found on the rocky coast.

Soups

and

Stews

OREGON COAST
AQUARIUM

Mo's® Seafood Cioppino

1/2 cup olive oil
2 green bell peppers, seeded and chopped
1 large yellow onion, chopped
5 cloves garlic, minced
3 green onions, chopped
1/4 cup chopped parsley
2 bay leaves
1-1/2 tablespoons salt
1 tablespoon black pepper
1 tablespoon rosemary

1 tablespoon thyme
3 cups canned sliced mushrooms with their
   liquid
3 cups tomato puree
3 cups tomato sauce
1 cup red wine
1 cup water
3 pounds seafood such as white fish, salmon,
   oysters, shellfish or a mixture of all

In a large pot, heat olive oil over medium heat. Add green bell peppers, onion, and garlic and sauté until barely tender. Add green onions, parsley, bay leaves, salt, pepper, rosemary, and thyme and stir to mix well. Add mushrooms, tomato puree, tomato sauce, wine and water and bring to a boil. Reduce heat to low, cover and simmer 30 minutes, stirring often.

Add seafood of your choice, cover and simmer until seafood is cooked through, about 15 minutes. Serves 8.

Cindy McEntee
Mo's® Enterprises, Inc.

Fish Stock

2 pounds fish trimmings (heads, bones and
   tails)
2 quarts water
1 onion, sliced
2 stalks celery, cut into thirds

2 tablespoons chopped parsley
1 clove garlic
1 bay leaf
5 peppercorns
1 teaspoon salt

In a large pot, combine all ingredients and bring to a boil. Reduce heat to low, cover and simmer 30 minutes. Strain stock and discard the solids. Makes about 12 cups.

Gage M. Burger

 *Salmon Chowder*

1 quart water
1 cup chopped onion
1/2 cup chopped celery
2 chicken bouillon cubes
1/2 teaspoon pepper
Salt to taste

3/4 pound salmon filet, boneless and skinless
4 slices bacon, chopped and partially cooked
6 potatoes, peeled and diced
1 cup half and half
Butter, minced chives or paprika

In a large pot, combine water, onion, celery, chicken bouillon, pepper, and salt and bring to a simmer over medium heat. Add salmon and poach for about 5 minutes, or until just cooked through. Remove salmon from stock and cool. Flake salmon into bite-sized pieces. Return salmon to pot and add partially cooked bacon and diced potatoes. Cook until potatoes are tender. Add half and half and heat through without boiling. Adjust seasonings and serve. Garnish with a dollop of butter, chives or paprika if desired. Serves 6 to 8.

Tina Retasket
Siletz Tribal Smokehouse

 Bouillabaisse à la Kernville

1/4 cup olive oil
1 onion, diced
1 green bell pepper, seeded and diced
1 red bell pepper, seeded and diced
2 stalks celery, chopped
3 tablespoons chopped parsley
2 tablespoons minced garlic
2 tablespoons Italian seasoning
1 tablespoon black pepper
4 cups water
1 (16-ounce) can whole tomatoes

1 (14-ounce) bottle ketchup
1/4 cup dry white wine
1 tablespoon sugar
1 teaspoon chili powder
1 teaspoon thyme
5 pounds steamer clams
3 pounds crab legs
1 pound halibut, cut into bite-sized pieces
24 scallops
16 shucked oysters
16 prawns

In a large pot, heat olive oil over medium heat. Add, onion, green bell pepper, red bell pepper, celery, parsley, garlic, Italian seasoning, and black pepper and sauté until just tender. Stir in water, tomatoes, ketchup, wine, sugar, chili powder, and thyme and bring to a boil over high heat. As soon as mixture starts boiling, reduce heat to medium and simmer 5 minutes.

Add clams, crab, halibut, scallops, oysters, and prawns. Cover and simmer 10 to 15 minutes, stirring often, until clams open and fish is cooked through. Discard any unopened clams. Serves 8.

Anthony Danna
Kernville Steak and Seafood Restaurant

Trout House Fisherman's Stew in Rich Tomato Broth

4 cups clam juice
4 cups diced tomatoes and their juice
1 cup dry white wine
2 tablespoons lemon juice
2 tablespoons Worcestershire sauce
1 tablespoon minced garlic
1 tablespoon basil
1 teaspoon marjoram
1 teaspoon tarragon
2 bay leaves
2 tablespoons olive oil
2 stalks celery, diced
1 medium carrot, diced

16 steamer clams
Flour for dusting
8 ounces cod OR halibut, cut into 1/2-inch
 cubes
8 prawns, peeled and deveined
6 ounces sea scallops
1 bunch green onions, finely chopped
1 cup loosely packed parsley, chopped
4 ounces bay shrimp
2 ounces crab meat
2 tablespoons butter
Salt and pepper to taste

In a large pot, combine clam juice, tomatoes and their juice, wine, lemon juice, Worcestershire sauce, garlic, basil, marjoram, tarragon, and bay leaves and bring to a boil. Reduce heat to low and simmer for 1 hour.

In a large skillet, heat olive oil over medium heat. Add celery, carrot, and clams. Sauté until clams begin to open. Lightly dust cod, prawns, and scallops with flour. Add to skillet and lightly brown on all sides.

Add mixture in skillet to the tomato mixture in the large pot and simmer until the seafood is just cooked through. Add green onions, parsley, bay shrimp, crab meat, and butter to the pot and cook until heated through. Season with salt and pepper. Serves 6.

Matthew Thompson, Chef
Trout House Restaurant

In the Rocks

Like many people, wolf-eels prefer cracked crab to fish. They use their buck teeth and strong jaws to crush crabs, sea urchins and other shellfish. When not out hunting, the wolf-eels' long, spotted, gray-green bodies nearly disappear into cracks in the rocks.

Despite their fierce, toothsome looks, wolf-eels are caring parents when compared to many fishes. the female lays her eggs in a rocky cave and both parents guard the eggs until they hatch.

All eels are fish but not all "eels" are eels. Take, for example, the wolf-eel. This fish was named for its sinuous, eel-like body. And since it hasn't got much of a tail, it even swims like an eel, flexing in waves down the length of its body.

But it takes more than body shape and swimming style to make an eel. True eels have spineless fins and small gill openings. Wolf-eels have flexible fin spines and quite large gills. So, despite deceiving looks and name, the wolf-eel is not really an eel.

 *Billi Bi Soup*

3-1/2 pounds mussels, scrubbed and
    debearded
1 cup dry white wine
1 stalk celery, chopped
1 small onion, chopped

1 bay leaf
1/2 teaspoon thyme
Water to cover
1 quart heavy cream

Place mussels, wine, celery, onion, bay leaf, thyme and enough water to cover in a large pot. Bring to a boil then reduce heat to medium-low and simmer gently for 45 minutes.

Strain mixture and reserve mussels for another use. Discard shells and vegetables. Return stock to pot and reduce to about 3 cups. Stock will taste very strong. Add cream and bring to a boil then reduce to medium and simmer for 5 minutes. Serves 4.

Chris Pontrelli and Jim Burley

Pacific Seafood Chowder

Looking for a hearty chowder? Try combining the best seafood the Pacific Northwest has to offer.

1/4 cup butter
2 medium yellow onions, diced
1 large potato, peeled and diced
1 carrot, peeled and diced
1 stalk celery, diced
8 ounces wild mushrooms such as chantrelles,
    morels, or shiitakes, sliced
4 cups clam juice
1 cup dry white wine
2 tablespoons chopped Italian parsley

1 sprig fresh thyme
8 ounces chopped clams, canned or fresh
8 ounces mussels in shells
8 ounces shucked oysters with juice
8 ounces halibut filets; skinned, boned and
    cut into 1-inch cubes
8 ounces salmon filets; skinned, boned, and
    cut into 1-inch cubes
1 cup heavy cream
Salt and pepper to taste

Melt butter in large Dutch oven, preferably cast iron, over medium heat. Add onions, potato, carrot and celery and sauté for 5 minutes without browning. Add clam juice, wine, Italian parsley and thyme and bring to a boil. Reduce heat to medium-low and simmer for 10 minutes. Add clams, mussels, oysters, halibut and salmon and simmer for about 15 minutes or until fish starts to fall apart. Add cream and salt and pepper to taste. Heat through and ladle into soup bowl while piping hot. Serves 6 to 8.

Alfred Popp

Bouillabaisse

3 quarts fish stock
3 cups chopped tomatoes
1 cup dry sherry
1/4 cup chopped garlic
1 tablespoon minced fresh basil
1 tablespoon lobster base (optional)
1-1/2 teaspoons thyme
5 stalks celery, chopped
1 bunch leeks (white and pale green parts
    only), cleaned well and chopped

1 large yellow onion, chopped
1/2 teaspoon saffron
18 steamer clams
8 ounces halibut, cut into bite-sized pieces
8 ounces salmon, cut into bite-sized pieces
8 prawns
8 scallops
2 cups bay shrimp
12 crab legs
Salt and pepper to taste

In a large pot, combine fish stock, tomatoes, sherry, garlic, basil, lobster base, and thyme and bring to a boil. Reduce heat to low, cover and simmer 1 hour.

Add celery, leeks, onion, and saffron and simmer 5 minutes. Add halibut, salmon, prawns, and scallops and simmer until fish is cooked, about 10 minutes. Stir in bay shrimp and crab legs and simmer until heated through. Season with salt and pepper to taste. Serve in large bowls. Serves 6.

Gracie's at Smuggler's Cove

"Dan & Louis Oyster Bar"
Oyster Stew

As served at Dan & Louis Oyster Bar in Portland, Oregon for over 85 years.

1 gallon milk
2 tablespoons butter
2 teaspoons salt
2 teaspoons Schilling Seasonall salt

1/8 teaspoon pepper
2 pounds shucked Yaquina Bay oysters
Butter for garnish, about 5 tablespoons
Oyster crackers

In the top of a large double-boiler, heat milk over simmering water until bubbles form on top of milk, about 30 minutes. Add 2 tablespoons butter, salt, Seasonall salt, and pepper and stir vigorously. Add raw oysters and stir. When most of the oysters have floated to the surface, or when most of the edges of the oysters curl, remove oysters with a slotted spoon and divide among 10 large bowls. Ladle hot stew milk into the bowls. Garnish with 1/2 tablespoon butter per bowl. Serve with oyster crackers. Serves 10.

Dan & Louis Oyster Bar Restaurant

Giant Pacific Octopus

Eight arms, two keen eyes and a baggy red body add up to a giant Pacific octopus, not a sea monster. Despite its fearsome reputation, the octopus is quite shy, sleeping by day in a rocky den or crevice to hide from predators.

By night, the octopus combs the seafloor seeking crabs, shrimp and other shellfish. After collecting an armload, the octopus returns to the privacy of its den, eats its fill and piles the empty shells outside in what's called an octopus's garden.

Although it's spineless, the octopus has quite a brain. Encased in a skull made of cartilage, the octopus's brain is similar to a vertebrate's brain. In fact, the octopus and its relative the squid are the only invertebrates known to sleep regularly.

Studies of behavior and brain structure in octopuses show they can remember, learn and cope well with new situations. Some scientists consider the octopus to be as intelligent as another puss—the common house cat.

Usually solitary, octopuses come together to breed. The male's third arm on the right is designed to deliver sperm packets to the female. Mating can take hours. Afterwards, the male octopus goes his way, leaving the female to find a nursery cave.

The female octopus lays up to 80,000 rice-sized eggs, hanging them from the ceiling of her cave in strings. She seldom eats during the five to six months she cares for her eggs and dies soon after they hatch. On average, only two of her young will live to adulthood.

When faced with a hungry lingcod, an octopus tries first to fade into the scenery by changing its color to match its background. If that doesn't work, the octopus squirts a blob of dark ink at the fish and disappears in a black cloud.

An octopus captures a crab or other prey with its tentacles, bites the crab with its sharp parrot-like beak, injecting it with poison. Then it floods its prey with digestive juices and sucks out the partly digested meat.

Without a protective shell, the octopus has become a master of disguise. Special pigment cells and muscles match its color and texture to the surroundings. Usually reddish brown and wrinkly, the octopus can range from dark red to off-white and from bumpy to smooth.

The octopus gets a grip on things with eight muscular arms or tentacles, each covered with a double row of about 240 suction cups. Using arms and suckers, an octopus feels in rocky cracks and crevices in search of food.

The octopus has well-developed eyes for an invertebrate, similar in structure to a mammal's. Its vision is so good it can judge the distance and speed of moving prey and easily snatch up crabs as they scuttle for cover.

When moving slowly, an octopus pulls itself arm-over-arm along the bottom. But when there's a need for speed, the octopus uses jet propulsion. It squirts water out of a tube in one direction which pushes it quickly in the opposite direction.

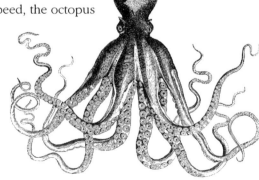

Mo's® Oyster Stew

16 ounces shucked Pacific OR kumomoto
    oysters
1 teaspoon salt

1/4 teaspoon pepper
4 tablespoons butter
6 cups milk

Place oysters in a medium saucepan. Add salt and pepper. Barely cover with water and bring to a boil. Remove from heat and cool. Larger oysters should be cut into bite-sized pieces and returned to the oysters and their broth.

Divide oysters and their broth evenly into 4 large bowls. Top each with 1 tablespoon butter. In a medium saucepan, bring milk just to a boil and pour over oysters. Serves 4.

Cindy McEntee
Mo's® Enterprises, Inc.

Seafood Gumbo

1 cup olive oil
8 cups chopped celery
8 cups chopped onions
4 cups chopped lettuce
2 cups shredded carrots
2 cups chopped leeks (white and pale green
    parts only)
1-1/2 cloves elephant garlic, chopped
2 tablespoons gumbo seasoning
1 tablespoon basil
1 tablespoon thyme
1 teaspoon anise seed OR fennel
12 peppercorns
3 bay leaves

3 gallons chicken stock
1 (10-pound) can tomatoes
2 cups dry white wine
1 pound okra, cut into 2-inch pieces
1 pound salmon, cut into bite-sized pieces
1 pound skate, cut into bite-sized pieces
1 pound tuna, cut into bite-sized pieces
1 pound scallops
1 pound bay shrimp
Salt and pepper to taste
Cayenne pepper to taste
2 quarts steamer clams, scrubbed
Chopped parsley for garnish

In a very large pot, heat olive oil over medium heat. Add onions, celery, lettuce, carrots, leeks, garlic, gumbo seasoning, basil, thyme, anise, peppercorns, and bay leaves and sauté until tender.

Add chicken stock, tomatoes, wine, okra, salmon, skate, tuna, scallops, bay shrimp, salt, pepper, and cayenne and bring to a boil over medium-high heat. When mixture comes to a boil, reduce heat to low, cover and simmer 3 hours, stirring often.

Before serving, stir in steamers and simmer until they open. Discard any unopened clams. Garnish with parsley and serve. Serves 25.

Chez Claudine French-American
Restaurant

Papa's Cioppino

4 tablespoons olive oil
1 large onion, chopped
2 cloves garlic, minced
1 (6-pound-6-ounce) can tomatoes
2 cups dry white wine
1 tablespoon sugar
1 teaspoon basil
1 teaspoon oregano
1 teaspoon salt

1 bay leaf
1/4 teaspoon black pepper
1/8 teaspoon dried hot red chile flakes
3 pounds cleaned squid, body sliced into rings
    and tentacles cut into bite-sized pieces
2 pounds shelled and deveined shrimp
2 Dungeness crabs, legs broken off and body
    separated into 4 pieces
1 pound rockfish, cut into bite-sized pieces

In a large pot, heat olive oil over medium heat. Add onion and garlic and sauté until tender. Add tomatoes, wine, sugar, basil, oregano, salt, bay leaf, pepper, and dried chile flakes and stir well, breaking up tomatoes. Reduce heat to low, cover, and simmer for 1 hour, stirring occasionally.

Stir in squid, shrimp, crabs, and rock fish and simmer until seafood is cooked through, about 15 minutes. Serve with lots of French or Italian bread. Serves 8 to 10.

Chris Pontrelli

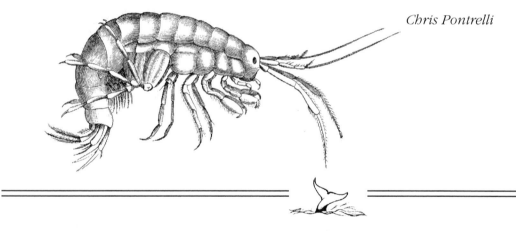

On a Rocky Reef

Reefs are rocky, dark and deep

    Deep reefs rise up from the continental shelf, breaking the monotony of the flat seafloor. The water is calm, too deep to be stirred by restless surface waves. Anemones and other animals encrust the rocks but the light isn't strong enough for most seaweeds to grow.

    Juvenile rockfish take refuge along the reef where open water predators can't maneuver well. Adult fish, too, find shelter here, as well as food in the form of crabs, sea urchins and other edible animals.

Why do a fish's eyes bulge when you reel it up?

    When you reel up a fish, the water pressure on its body decreases and the gas in its swim bladder expands. The fish can't compensate so the bladder blows up like a balloon, filling the fish's body and making its eyes bulge.

Sea Hag Bouillabaisse

2 tablespoons olive oil
1 bunch leeks (white and pale green parts
    only), cleaned and chopped
1/4 cup minced garlic
1/4 cup minced shallots
1 gallon fish stock
2 (15-ounce) cans plum tomatoes
8 tomatoes, peeled and chopped
1 cup dry white wine
4 bay leaves
1-1/2 tablespoons basil
1-1/2 tablespoons thyme
Fish bouillon concentrate to taste (optional)

Lobster base to taste (optional)
4 cups chopped onion
2 cups chopped celery
2 pounds halibut OR cod, cut into 1-inch
    pieces
1-1/4 pounds salmon, cut into 1-inch pieces
50 steamer clams, scrubbed
40 sea scallops
30 jumbo prawns, peeled and deveined
24 Dungeness crab legs
1 pound bay shrimp
Chopped parsley for garnish

In a large pot, heat olive oil over medium heat. Add leeks, garlic, and shallots and sauté until just tender. Add fish stock, plum tomatoes, tomatoes, wine, bay leaves, basil, thyme, fish bouillon concentrate, and lobster base and simmer 15 minutes, stirring often. Reduce heat to low and stir in onion, celery, halibut, salmon, clams, scallops, prawns, and crab and cover pot. Simmer until fish is cooked and clams open, about 3 to 5 minutes. Remove from heat and stir in bay shrimp. Serve in a very large heavy bowl garnished with chopped parsley. Provide damp finger towels and a crab cracker. Enjoy! Serves 12.

Lorna K. Weller
Sea Hag Restaurant and Lounge

Striped bass
(Morone saxatilis)

Striped bass were introduced here from the East Coast. Like salmon, these bass usually live at sea and return to freshwater rivers to spawn. But some striped bass introduced into landlocked rivers and lakes live out their entire lives in fresh water.

Sturgeon

Feeding on shrimps, clams and worms, sturgeon grow slowly as they swim about in murky bays and estuaries. Slow as they may be, sturgeon have been known to grow 20 feet long in a life span of more than 80 years.

Slow-growing sturgeon aren't quick to mature. White sturgeon take 11 years to reach adulthood and even then, they may wait four to 11 years between spawning. But what the sturgeon lack in frequency, they make up for in quantity, laying as many as 4.7 million eggs.

Sea Hag Clam Chowder

3 (6-1/2-ounce) cans chopped clams
4 (8-ounce) bottles clam juice
1 tablespoon Minor's Clam Base (optional)
1/4 teaspoon basil
1/4 teaspoon thyme
3/4 cup butter
1 cup flour
8 ounces bacon, chopped

3/4 cup chopped celery
3/4 cup chopped onion
3 cups peeled and diced potatoes
4 cups scalded milk OR half and half
Butter and chopped parsley

Drain clams, reserving juice, and set aside. Combine reserved clam juice, bottled clam juice, Minor's Clam Base, basil, and thyme in a large pot and bring to a simmer over medium heat.

In a small saucepan, melt butter over medium-low heat. Whisk in flour to make a roux. Cook, stirring often, for about 20 minutes.

In a skillet, cook bacon over medium heat until slightly brown on the edges. Discard bacon grease. Add celery and onions and sauté until barely tender.

In a medium saucepan, bring 2 quarts of salted water to a boil. Cook diced potatoes in boiling water until just tender. Drain and set aside.

Whisk 1 cup of simmering clam juice mixture into roux until smooth. Pour into remaining clam juice mixture, whisking constantly, until thoroughly blended. Stir in clams, bacon mixture, and potatoes and bring back to a boil. Reduce heat to low and stir in scalded milk and heat through but do not let boil. Garnish with a dollop of butter and chopped parsley. Serves 6 to 8.

Lorna K. Weller
Sea Hag Restaurant and Lounge

Cioppino

There are many variations of this noble dish. Through trials and tribulations and many refinements, this version has become a top seller at Seafood Mama Restaurant.

1/4 cup olive oil
3 stalks celery, chopped
1 onion, diced
1 green bell pepper, seeded and diced
1-1/2 cups sliced mushrooms
2 cloves garlic, minced
1/4 teaspoon minced parsley
2 tomatoes, peeled and diced
3 tablespoons tomato paste
8 cups fish stock
1 cup red wine
Salt and pepper to taste
1/4 teaspoon basil

1/4 teaspoon oregano
8 ounces salmon, cut into 1-inch pieces
8 ounces white fish, cut into 1-inch pieces
8 steamer clams, scrubbed
8 mussels, scrubbed and debearded
8 prawns, shelled but tails left on
4 crab legs
4 crawfish
4 scallops
6 ounces bay shrimp

In a large pot, heat olive oil over medium heat. Add celery, onion, green bell pepper, mushrooms, garlic, and parsley and sauté until tender. Stir in tomatoes, tomato paste, fish stock, wine, salt, pepper, basil, and oregano. Reduce heat to medium-low, cover, and simmer for 20 minutes.

Add salmon, white fish, clams, mussels, prawns, crab, crawfish, and scallops. Cover and continue cooking, stirring often, until fish is cooked and clams and mussels are open. Discard any unopened clams or mussels.

To serve, place in large soup bowl and top with bay shrimp. Be sure to have the crawfish, crab legs and prawns extending from the bowl for eye appeal. Serve this tasty dish with a great Oregon red wine and crusty garlic bread. Serves 4.

Jack Koberstein
Seafood Mama Restaurant

Barnacles

It's hard to believe, but barnacles are related to crabs and shrimp. Tucked inside their fortressed shells, they weather the roughest waves. But when the tide's in, their feathery feet are out, grabbing at food drifting by.

Barnacles go through a free-swimming stage as larva. Many other species also start out as planktonic larvae that don't look or act anything like adults. Eventually they grow up to be responsible crabs, snails, lobsters and fish.

Oyster and Corn Chowder
for New Year's Eve

*I made this recipe for a shared vineyard and winemaker families New Year's gathering.
I wanted to use oysters, but also wanted something more. The result was filling and pretty tasty!
Serve with warm French bread and Pinot Gris.*

4 cups milk
2 pints shucked oysters, with their liquid
1/2 cup butter
1/4 teaspoon cayenne pepper
1 tablespoon olive oil
2 medium onions, diced
2 leeks, white part only, chopped

2 cloves garlic, minced
2 teaspoons minced fresh thyme
6 cups peeled and diced potatoes
2 (10-ounce) packages frozen corn
**1 bunch spinach, washed well and sliced in
    2-inch strips**
Salt and pepper to taste

Place milk, oysters, butter, and cayenne in the top of a double boiler. Heat over simmering water until oysters curl around the edges and butter has melted. If oysters are very large, cut them into bite-sized pieces. Set aside.

In a large pot, heat olive oil over medium heat. Add onions, leeks, garlic, and thyme and sauté until translucent and lightly browned.

In another large pot, cook potatoes in boiling salted water until tender. Add corn and bring back to a boil. Remove from heat and stir in spinach. When spinach begins to wilt, drain and discard liquid.

Combine the above ingredients and bring to a bare simmer to heat through. Season to taste with salt and pepper. Serves 10 to 12.

Marilyn Webb
Bethel Heights Vineyard

Ochre star (pisaster ochraceus)

If you see a star on the rocky shore, whether purple, orange, or brown, chances are it's an ochre star. No one knows why they come in so many colors, or why orange stars are more common on rough coasts, and purple ones are more common on calmer shores.

Oregon hairy triton (fusitriton oregonensis)

The Oregon hairy triton lays egg cases that look like spiral clusters of corn. Each "kernel" holds hundreds of eggs. The first snails to hatch in each case eat up all their unhatched brothers and sisters. How's that for sibling rivalry?

Brodetto di Portorecanti

One of my fondest memories in Italy was staying with the Polzonetti family in Fabriano and tasting Nauda's delicious brodetto. I hold this family dear to my heart and will always be grateful for their gracious hospitality. She was so kind to share the history and recipe for this traditional dish with me.

Brodetto di Portorecanti is an ancient dish from the Marche region in central Italy. The number of fish varies but should not have 13 different kinds since an old tradition says that Jesus had brodetto for the last supper and he wanted 13 varieties to represent his disciples. Now it is best not to use 13 kinds because one fish will represent Judas.

3 tablespoons olive oil
1 onion, finely chopped
3 tablespoons minced fresh parsley
2 cloves garlic, minced
1/4 cup dry white wine
1/4 cup white wine vinegar
1 cup tomato sauce
3 pounds assorted fish, such as halibut, sea
    bass, red snapper, cod, shark, and salmon,
    cut into 2-inch pieces

1 pound assorted shellfish, such as rock
    shrimp, mussels, lobster, prawns,
    and clams
6 slices crostini (French or Italian bread,
    brushed with olive oil and toasted)

In a large pot, heat olive oil over medium heat. Add onion, parsley, and garlic and sauté until onion is translucent. Add wine and vinegar and reduce by half. Add tomato sauce and reduce heat to low. Add fish, cover and simmer 15 minutes. Add shellfish, cover and simmer an additional 15 minutes.

Place crostini in the bottom of 6 large bowls. Top with the brodetto. Serve with a chilled Italian white wine such as a Verdicchio. Serves 6.

Nauda Polzonetti
Pier Paolo Polzonetti
Patricia Wied

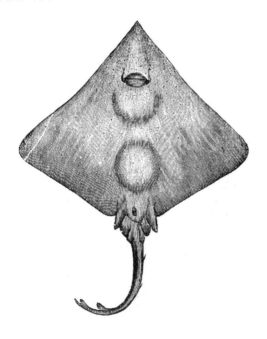

Coastal Waters Stories

Don't be alarmed if it loses an arm

Encircled by five arms, brittle stars look much like their relatives, the sea stars. But brittle star bodies are small and round, and their arms are skinny and spiny, adept at catching food out of water and on the bottom.

Brittle stars earned their name the hard way. If an arm is captured, it breaks off, leaving the arm to occupy the predator. Meanwhile, the rest of the star crawls under a rock to regrow the lost limb.

Sex isn't straightforward in the sea

Pandulus shrimps like the spot prawn and coon-stripe shrimp live throughout the eastern Pacific. Both sexes are brightly colored with spots and stripes across their bodies, legs and antennae.

The males are smaller than the females, though, and for years fishermen asked scientists why. The surprising answer is these shrimp all start out as males. Then, after two and a half years, they change sex and become females.

Cancer crabs are real house hunters

Round, dark-red Oregon cancer crabs like to snuggle into holes just their size. Smaller than the palm of your hand, these crabs build caves under loose rocks or in kelp holdfasts. They also move into holes in sandstone left behind by sea urchins.

When other housing is scarce, these little crabs search out the right-sized giant acorn barnacles, crush the living barnacles with their strong claws and eat them. Then the crabs move into the newly vacated shells.

The net result is slime

Sticky, toxic slime from glands along its sides is a hagfish's first line of defense. A disturbed hagfish quickly coats itself in ooze. At times, the slime is too much even for the hagfish. It ties itself in a knot that slides down its body and scrapes the ooze away.

Hagfish are especially annoying to commercial fishermen. These scavengers damage the fish trapped in their nets. When the nets are pulled aboard, the hagfish ooze bucketfuls of sticky slime all over the nets, fish and fishermen alike.

Hagfish go in for dinner

On the deep, dark seafloor, the primitive hagfish's eyes aren't much good for finding prey. Instead, this scavenger seeks dead or dying fish with its keen sense of smell. To stake its claim, the hagfish may cover its meal with a glaze of slime.

The hagfish eats from the inside out, tearing off chunks of its prey with a toothy tongue and a hard plate on the roof of its mouth. When dinner's over, all that's left of the fish is a bag of skin and bones.

Open sea fish hide in plain sight

Fish often have dark backs and pale, silvery sides and bellies, a color pattern called countershading. Seen from above, the dark backs merge with the deepening water. Seen from below, the pale sides and belly blend in with the light streaming down from the surface.

Both freshwater and ocean-going fish may be countershaded, especially those that live near the surface. Herring are countershaded to help conceal them from predators like tuna. And the tuna are countershaded as well, to conceal them from their predators: sharks and orcas.

Coastal Waters

OREGON COAST AQUARIUM

"There is one knows not what sweet mystery about this sea, whose . . . stirrings seem to speak of some hidden soul beneath."

Herman Melville

Jellyfish provide the centerpiece for the Coastal Waters Gallery, occupying an acrylic cylinder eight feet in diameter. The moon jellies exhibited are consistently named by our visitors as one of the most popular animals at the Aquarium. A second permanent jellyfish exhibit features sea nettles. Other gallery highlights include a 5,000-gallon kelp forest harboring small off-shore fishes in bull kelp, and a 9,100-gallon coastal reef exhibit. The gallery holds a total of 15 separate exhibits.

Animals exhibited in the Coastal Waters Gallery include basket stars, ratfish, rockfishes, and a variety of deeper water fishes and invertebrates.

Pasta
and
Rice

OREGON COAST
AQUARIUM

Granchio
(Crab Cappelini)

This is one of our all time favorites. We put it on the menu three years ago and it's always in demand as long as crab is in season.

2 tablespoons olive oil
5 large shallots, sliced
3/4 teaspoon salt
1/4 teaspoon pepper
2 Roma tomatoes, chopped
16 large fresh basil leaves, sliced
3/4 cup dry white wine

6 ounces crab meat
1/4 cup freshly grated Parmesan cheese
4 ounces cappellini OR angel hair pasta,
　　cooked in boiling salted water until
　　al dente then drained
Chopped parsley and additional Parmesan
　　cheese

In a large skillet, heat olive oil over high heat. When hot but not smoking add shallots, salt and pepper and sauté, stirring constantly, until shallots are brown and crispy, about 5 minutes. Take care not to burn shallots. Add tomatoes, basil and wine, reduce heat to medium and simmer until mixture has reduced by two-thirds. Stir in crab and heat through. Add cooked and drained pasta and 1/4 cup Parmesan and toss gently but thoroughly. When pasta is well coated with sauce, divide onto 2 plates. Garnish with parsley and additional Parmesan. Serves 2.

Lydia Bugatti and John Cress
Bugatti's Ristorante

Seafood Pasta

5 tablespoons butter
1 medium onion, diced
1/2 cup diced celery
1/4 cup flour
2 cups milk

1 cup cooked and flaked salmon
1/2 cup Dungeness crab meat
1/2 cup bay shrimp
4 cups cooked corkscrew pasta

In a skillet, melt 1 tablespoon butter over medium heat. Add onion and celery and sauté until translucent. Set aside.

In a medium saucepan, melt remaining 4 tablespoons butter over medium heat. Whisk in flour and cook, stirring constantly, for about 1 minute. Pour in milk slowly, while whisking to prevent any lumps. Cook, continuing to whisk, until mixture begins to thicken. Stir in reserved onion mixture, salmon, crab, and shrimp. Simmer until heated through. Remove from heat and toss with cooked pasta. Serves 4.

Tina Retasket
Siletz Tribal Smokehouse

Jellyfish

What is a jellyfish?

Despite their common name, jellies aren't fish. They float through life with no brain, no spine, no bones and no heart. In fact, these animals are actually more than 95 percent water and salts.

Jellies swim by contracting the band of muscle fibers encircling the bell. Because this gentle pulsing isn't very strong, jellies are considered part of the plankton, a group of organisms that drift with the currents. There, they play an important role as predators.

Recipe for home-made jellies

In summer when food and water conditions are right, mature male moon jellies broadcast sperm to fertilize eggs produced by females. The eggs are then brooded along the females' mouth arms. When the eggs hatch into larvae, they swim off to settle on a hard surface.

Once settled, the larvae become polyps which actually look more like minute sea anemones than jellies. In time, the polyps divide into many tiny flat jellies stacked up like plates. As they mature, the young jellies leave the stack to grow into the familiar bell-shaped adults.

Not all jellies . . .

Not all jellies look like the everyday, transparent, bell-shaped, tentacle-fringed type. They come in tints of red, purple, brown or blue. One kind may have short delicate tentacles while another has thick, muscular ones. Some jellies are longer than wide while some are nearly round.

As a group . . .

As a group, jellies are found all over the world from polar seas to tropical waters and from the surface to depths of 2,000 feet or more. Most are saltwater-dwellers, but a few species survive in freshwater lakes.

Of what possible use . . .

Of what possible use are jellies? Believe it or not, sea stars and blue rockfish eat them. Sea turtles sometimes mistake plastic bags for jellies, one of their favorite foods. And in China, Japan and Korea, salted and dried jellies are considered a delicacy for people, too.

True jellies . . .

True jellies aren't the only animals known as jellyfish. Hundred-foot-long Portuguese men-of-war and marble-sized sea gooseberries differ biologically from true jellies but they and others are called jellyfish because they are drifters with jelly-like bodies.

Organisms in open water . . .

Organisms in open water take cover where they can find it. For some kinds of tiny crabs and young fishes, the choice is clear. They live in jellies' bells and among their tentacles, gaining shelter from predators without affecting their hosts.

In general, a jelly has a bell-shaped body that may be clear or faintly colored. The jelly's stomach and sex organs are inside. Simple sensors along the bell's rim help the jelly orient itself to light and to the surface of the water. Tentacles and lacy mouth arms trail from the jelly's body. Covered with stinging cells, the tentacles stun or kill plankton and other small animals that touch them. Then the mouth arms carry the food upward to the jelly's stomach.

Linguini and Clams à la Yachats

1/2 cup butter
1/3 cup olive oil
1/2 cup chopped fresh parsley
2 cloves garlic, minced
1 (14-ounce) can whole tomatoes, chopped
1 tablespoon minced fresh basil
1/2 teaspoon oregano

1/4 teaspoon salt
1/8 teaspoon dried hot chile flakes
1/8 teaspoon black pepper
24 steamer clams in the shells
1/2 pound fresh clam meat, chopped
1 cup crab meat
12 ounces linguini

In a large skillet, heat the butter and olive oil together over medium heat. Add parsley and garlic and sauté until tender, about 5 minutes. Stir in tomatoes, basil, oregano, salt, hot chile flakes, and pepper. Cover and reduce heat to low. Simmer gently for about 15 minutes, stirring occasionally.

Place steamer clams in a large pot and add enough water until it comes up 1-inch. Cover tightly and bring to a boil over high heat. Steam until shells open. Remove clams with a slotted spoon and set aside. Strain the cooking liquid and reserve 1/2 cup of broth. Add the 1/2 cup broth to simmering tomato sauce.

Add the 1/2 pound of fresh clam meat and crab to the tomato sauce and simmer an additional 5 minutes.

Cook linguini in plenty of salted boiling water until al dente. Drain well. Pour pasta in a large serving dish and pour sauce over. Garnish with reserved steamer calms. Serves 4.

Chris Pontrelli

Rock Shrimp and Riesling

This easy to prepare rock shrimp and fettucine dish is a snap to make in the microwave.

1 pound fresh rock shrimp
1/4 cup Amity Dry Riesling
3 tablespoons olive oil

1 tablespoon lemon juice
1 pound fresh fettucine
Fresh Parmesan cheese for grating

Place rock shrimp in a single layer in a 9-inch microwave-safe baking dish. Combine Amity Dry Riesling, 2 tablespoons olive oil, and lemon juice and pour over rock shrimp. Cook on high for 4 minutes, or until shrimp have turned pink and are cooked through.

In a large pot, bring 5 quarts of water and the remaining 1 tablespoon olive together to a rolling boil. Stir in the fettucine and cook for 2 to 3 minutes or until al dente. Drain fettucine and toss with shrimp mixture in a large pasta bowl. Top with grated Parmesan cheese and serve with a green salad and the remaining Amity Dry Riesling.

Vicki Wettle
Amity Vineyards

Seafood Saffron Risotto
with Fennel and Roasted Peppers

4-1/2 cups clam juice
2 cups dry white wine
1 teaspoon saffron threads
6 tablespoons olive oil
10 ounces rock shrimp
8 ounces mussels, scrubbed and debearded
1 cup diced onions
1 fennel bulb, julienned
1 bunch fresh thyme (leaves only), minced

3 tablespoons chopped garlic
Zest of 1 lemon, minced
3 cups Arborio rice
Roasted Peppers (recipe follows)
2 tablespoons chopped fennel tops
1-2/3 cups freshly grated Parmesan cheese
6 tablespoons unsalted butter
Salt and pepper to taste

In a medium saucepan, combine clam juice, wine and saffron and simmer over low heat for 10 minutes.
In a large skillet, heat 3 tablespoons of the olive oil over medium heat. Add rock shrimp and mussels and sauté 6 minutes. Remove from heat and set aside.

In a medium pot, heat remaining 3 tablespoons olive oil over medium heat. Add onions and fennel and sauté until lightly browned. Add thyme, garlic, and lemon zest and sauté until fragrant. Add rice and stir until well coated with the olive oil.

Slowly stir in the hot clam juice mixture. Simmer over medium heat, stirring often, until liquid is almost absorbed, about 18 minutes. Stir in reserved seafood, roasted peppers, fennel tops, Parmesan, and butter. Simmer an additional 5 minutes, stirring often, to heat through. Season with salt and pepper to taste. Serves 6 to 8.

Roasted Peppers

2 tablespoons olive oil
3 red bell peppers

Preheat oven to 450 degrees. Lightly oil a baking sheet.

Cut peppers in half. Remove and discard seeds and veins. Place skin-side up on prepared baking sheet. Drizzle with olive oil. Roast until several black spots appear. Remove from oven and immediately place in a bowl and cover with plastic wrap. Let stand for 15 minutes. Remove and discard skin. Slice into strips.

Eugen Bingham
Il Piatto Restaurant

Paella

This is a traditional Spanish seafood, chicken and rice dish. It is a long recipe with several steps—however, it is not difficult.

1/2 cup hot water
1/2 teaspoon saffron threads
3 tablespoons olive oil
5 chorizo OR calabrese sausages, sliced into
    1/4-inch rounds
20 chicken drumettes OR 4 chicken breasts
    cut into long chunks
1 large onion, sliced
3 cloves garlic, minced
1 large red bell pepper, cut into strips
3 cups long-grain rice
3 cups chicken stock

4 tomatoes; peeled, seeded and chopped
2 tablespoons lemon juice
1 tablespoon paprika
Salt and pepper to taste
3 dozen steamer clams
20 to 30 medium shrimp, peeled
1 pound frozen peas, thawed
1 pound bay shrimp
1 cup black pitted olives, sliced
2 tomatoes, cut into wedges
2 lemons, cut into wedges

Preheat oven to 325 degrees.

Infuse the saffron by soaking it in the hot water. Set aside.

In a large oven-proof pot with a tight-fitting lid, heat the olive oil over medium heat. Add the sausage and cook until browned. Add chicken and cook until browned. Add onion and garlic, lower heat to medium-low, and cook until onion is softened. Add red pepper and stir mixture well. Raise heat to medium and add rice. Cook, stirring constantly, until rice is translucent. Add chicken stock, tomatoes, reserved saffron along with it's soaking liquid, lemon juice, paprika, salt, and pepper. Stir well to scrape up any browned bits on the bottom of pot and bring to a boil. Reduce heat to low, cover and simmer 10 minutes. Place covered pot into the oven and bake about 15 minutes, or until all liquid is absorbed by the rice.

While rice is cooking, bring a large pot of salted water to a boil. Drop in the clams and the medium shrimp. When the clams are open, and the shrimp turns pink, they are done. Discard any unopened clams. Drain in a colander and keep warm over hot water.

When rice mixture is done, remove from oven and stir in the peas, bay shrimp, and olives. Place on a large serving platter and arrange clams and shrimp on top. Garnish with tomato wedges and lemon wedges. Serve with a green salad, a fruit salad, crusty bread, and an Oregon white wine. Serves 10.

Joan MacDonald, Chef
University of Oregon Faculty Club

In a Kelp Forest

Kelp forests are food and shelter

Underwater forests of bull kelp sway gracefully, revealing and concealing the abundant life below. Shafts of sunlight pierce the cold water, touching a bat star here, a kelp crab there. Rockfish hang motionless in the shadow of the kelp blades.

The kelp forest provides shelter from the sea's constant surge. Small seaweeds grow like shrubs under the tall kelps. Well-camouflaged animals cling to the algae or lie flat against the bottom, their shapes and colors blending in with the seaweeds and rocks.

Sea urchins harvest the kelp forests

Under normal circumstances, sea urchins are content to eat drift algae: pieces of seaweeds that have broken off and are drifting in the currents. But if there are too many urchins in one area and not enough drift algae, urchins may go on the march in search of food.

A sea urchin will climb the base of a kelp plant and chew through the stipe, sometimes cutting the entire plant free. The kelp drifts out to sea or washes up on a beach. Either way, many scavengers including sea urchins make good use of the freed lunch.

How do seaweeds reproduce?

Seaweeds don't grow from seeds. Most large ones you see along the coast produce spores which grow into microscopic plants. These make eggs and sperm that join to produce the familiar large forms.

Seaweeds for all seasons

Some seaweeds, like bull kelp, have growing seasons. Lack of sunlight during the short winter days slows their growth and weakens them. Storm waves tear at the plants and the bobbing floats you see offshore in summer disappear. They wash up on the sand with other beach wrack.

But on the bottom, the bull kelp is busy producing the next generation. As the days get longer and the waves get gentler in spring, bull kelp begins to grow back and the forest returns.

Kelp Forest Zones

Kelp forests, like forests on land, grow in layers. Plants and animals in each layer are adapted to the living conditions there: light levels, wave surge, competition and predation. Big kelps, like tall forest trees, grow quickly to reach the sunny surface. Leaf-like blades form a roof, or canopy. Small fish hide there while snails and crabs graze on blades and stipes. Brown algae, like ferns and small trees in a forest, form a dense understory in shadowy light below the canopy. Shrubby, low-growing algae form the turf layer while flat coralline algae creep like moss over the seafloor. Crabs, brittle stars and others live in the tangled root-like holdfasts.

Holdfast

Name follows function in a bull kelp's holdfast. Its root-like branches grow over the rocks, wedging themselves into cracks and crevices. Firmly attached to the seafloor, the holdfast anchors the kelp against the pull of the waves.

Floats

Bull kelp has floats to keep its blades near the surface. Like little balloons, the floats are filled with a mixture of gases including nitrogen, oxygen and carbon monoxide.

Kelp Pickles

This recipe requires only seaweed from the beach and ingredients from any grocery store—no special canning equipment or experience needed! Gather firm, shiny bull kelp freshly washed up; it appears from time to time year round, and often after storms in the fall.

For each quart of pickles you want to make, take about 15 inches of stipe (the long, stem-like part) from the thicker end; you'll need more inches if you take from the thinner end.

Rinse the kelp. Slice it crosswise into 1-inch long circles. Simmer in water a few minutes to soften if you wish. Drain and pack into quart jars.

To each jar add:
    1-1/2 teaspoons pickling salt
    1/2 teaspoons pickling spices

and any of the following:
    1/4 cup sliced onion
    1 head fresh dill
    1 clove garlic, sliced
    1 small hot chile

Combine in a saucepan:
    1-3/4 cups cider vinegar
    3/4 cup water

Bring to a boil and fill the packed jar with the hot vinegar mixture. Wipe the rims of the jars and screw on the lids. Let the jars cool and store in the refrigerator for up to 6 weeks. Allow the pickles to sit for at least 1 week before opening.

Gelatin Diet Recipe
for Fishes and Invertebrates

This is a nutritious favorite of many of the fishes and invertebrates at the Oregon Coast Aquarium.

750 grams commercial trout or salmon feed
450 grams smelt or other fish
225 grams clam
225 grams krill or shrimp
225 grams spinach
225 grams carrots
1-1/2 tablespoons carophyll red
1-1/2 tablespoons beta carotene
20 ml aminoplex (amino acid/vitamin complex)

20 ml universal vitamin mix
10 ml HUFAs
2 tablespoons Stay C
36 (1/2-pound size) Mazuri fish vitamins, ground up
12 ounces Knox or food gelatin
1-1/2 liters very hot water

Completely thaw frozen ingredients and pour off water. Rinse krill until water is clear. Place all ingredients except gelatin and water in a large blender. Add 750 ml of the hot water to the blender and blend on low speed. Mix the gelatin with the remaining 750 ml hot water. Add the gelatin mixture to the blender and mix on high speed until smooth.

Pour the mixture into appropriate containers and refrigerate overnight. Gel that will not be used immediately should be frozen. Record date of manufacture and any additional ingredients on each container.

Animal Husbandry Staff
Oregon Coast Aquarium

Rigatoni Garibaldi

2 tablespoons olive oil
1/2 cup diced onion
1 tablespoon minced garlic
2-2/3 cups peeled and chopped tomatoes
8 ounces clam juice
1/8 teaspoon oregano

8 ounces bay shrimp
Salt and pepper to taste
1 pound rigatoni, cooked in boiling salted
    water until al dente then drained
Freshly grated Parmesan cheese

In a large saucepan, heat the olive oil over medium heat. Add the onion and garlic and sauté until just tender. Reduce heat to medium-low and add the tomatoes, simmer 5 minutes, stirring often. Add clam juice and oregano and simmer about 10 minutes. Add the bay shrimp and simmer an additional 5 minutes. Toss with the drained pasta. Serve with Parmesan cheese sprinkled on top. Serves 4.

Urbano Salvati, C.E.C.
Chef Instructor
Western Culinary Institute

 Fettucine with Mussels

4 tablespoons olive oil
1 small onion, diced
1 clove garlic, minced
1 (14-1/2-ounce) can Italian-style tomatoes
2 tablespoons chopped fresh parsley
1/4 teaspoon oregano

1/8 teaspoon basil
Salt and pepper
3 pounds fresh mussels, scrubbed and
    debearded
1 pound fettucine

Heat olive oil in a large skillet over medium heat. Add the onions and garlic and sauté until translucent. Stir in tomatoes, parsley, oregano, and basil. Reduce heat to low and simmer for 15 minutes.

Put mussels in a large pot. Add enough water until it comes up 1 inch. Cover tightly and bring to a boil over high heat. Shaking the pot occasionally, cook until mussels open. Discard any unopened mussels. Set aside 12 mussels to be used as garnish. Remove the meat from remaining mussels and stir into the tomato mixture. Strain 1/2 cup of the mussel cooking liquid and add to tomato mixture. Season with salt and pepper to taste. Heat through.

Cook fettucine in plenty of salted boiling water until al dente. Drain well. Pour pasta in a large serving dish and pour sauce over. Garnish with reserved mussels and serve. Serves 4 to 6.

Chris Pontrelli

Rock Shrimp and Scallop Risotto

7 tablespoons butter
4 cloves garlic, minced
8 ounces bay scallops
8 ounces rock shrimp
6 cups chicken stock
1 (15-ounce) can clam juice

1 cup dry white wine
1 medium onion, diced
1 medium red bell pepper, diced
2 cups Arborio rice
1/2 cup freshly grated Parmesan cheese
1/2 cup freshly grated Romano cheese

In a large skillet, melt 2 tablespoons butter and sauté 2 cloves garlic over medium heat until fragrant. Add scallops and shrimp and sauté just until shrimp starts to turn pink, do not overcook. Remove scallops and shrimp with a slotted spoon and set aside. Pour cooking juices into a large saucepan. Add chicken stock, clam juice, and wine and simmer over medium heat for about 10 minutes.

Return skillet to stove and melt remaining 4 tablespoons butter over medium heat. Add remaining 2 cloves garlic, onion, and red pepper and sauté until tender, about 5 minutes. Stir in rice until it is well coated with butter.

Begin adding the simmering stock to the rice mixture 1-1/2 cups at a time, stirring constantly. When the stock is almost absorbed by the rice, add another 1-1/2 cups of the simmering stock. Continue until the rice is cooked al dente.

When rice is tender but still a little firm, stir in the reserved scallops and shrimp. Sprinkle with Parmesan and Romano cheeses and serve immediately. Serves 6.

Kathy Goans
Tualatin Vineyards

Turtles

The painted turtle lives in sloughs, streams and rivers from western Washington and Oregon to Baja California. It feeds on plants and small animals, grows up to seven inches long and can live for more than 20 years.

More than 60 bones make up a turtle's shell, top and bottom. It's all covered by a layer of horny sections called scutes. When the turtle is attacked, it pulls its head and legs in and sits tight until the coast is clear.

Mussels Marsala

36 mussels, scrubbed and debearded
4 tablespoons olive oil
1/2 cup sliced mushrooms
1 tablespoon chopped parsley
1 clove garlic, minced
1/2 teaspoon salt
1/4 teaspoon basil
1/8 teaspoon dried hot red chile flakes

1/8 teaspoon pepper
1/4 cup dry Marsala
8 ounces penne pasta, cooked in boiling salted
    water until al dente then drained
1/4 cup seasoned dry bread crumbs

In a large pot, bring 3 cups of water to a boil over high heat. Add mussels and cover pot tightly. Steam about 5 to 7 minutes, or until mussels open. Discard any unopened mussels. Set aside 6 mussels in the shell for garnish. Remove remaining mussels from shells and set aside.

In a large skillet, heat olive oil over medium heat. Add mushrooms, parsley, garlic, salt, basil, chile flakes, and pepper and sauté until mushrooms are tender. Add Marsala and simmer 2 minutes. Add reserved mussel meat and heat through. Serve over cooked pasta. Sprinkle bread crumbs over the top and garnish with reserved mussels in shells. Serves 2.

Chris Pontrelli and Jim Burly

Moules Au Saffron

3 cups water
4 pounds mussels, scrubbed and debearded
1/4 teaspoon saffron threads
2 tablespoons unsalted butter
1 medium onion, finely chopped
1 tablespoon flour
1 cup heavy cream

1/4 teaspoon pepper
2 tablespoons chopped parsley
1 tablespoon Dijon mustard
1/2 teaspoon coriander
1 pound linguini, cooked in boiling salted
    water until al dente then drained

In a large pot, bring water to a boil over high heat. Add mussels and cover pot tightly. Steam about 5 to 7 minutes, or until mussels open. Discard any unopened mussels. Remove mussels with a slotted spoon and reserve 12 in the shell for garnish. Remove remaining mussels and set aside.

Save 2 cups of the mussel cooking liquid and strain through a coffee filter. Place in a small saucepan and bring to a boil over medium-high heat. Reduce liquid to 1/2 cup. Remove from heat and stir in saffron. Set aside.

In a large skillet, melt butter over medium heat. Add onions and sauté until onions are translucent. Sprinkle flour over onions and whisk until blended. Whisk in cream, pepper, and reduced mussel-saffron liquid. Reduce heat to low and simmer 15 minutes. Whisk in parsley, Dijon mustard, and coriander and simmer 3 minutes. Serve over pasta and garnish with reserved mussels in the shells. Serves 4.

Chris Pontrelli and Jim Burley

Oregon Frogs

Oregon is home to 11 species of frogs and toads.
Some are specialists, and some can live most anywhere.

Pacific Tree Frogs

Here's a frog that migrated to Hollywood. Those nighttime choruses on the soundtracks are usually Pacific tree frogs. In real life, males congregate in ponds all over the Northwest and call to attract females. Tree frogs cling as they climb. Many use special pads at the ends of their fingers and toes. Mucus oozes out between separated cells, and surface tension makes all 18 toepads stick tight.

Bullfrogs

The bullfrog thrives far from its original range—sometimes at the expense of other animals' survival. Bullfrogs were introduced into Oregon in the 1930s by people who must have liked their sound—and their taste. But the bullfrog has become a pest here, eating most anything it can get into its mouth, including native frogs and turtles.

Frog Development

The main way frogs survive is to lay lots of eggs—thousands and thousands of them. To start new frogs, a male and a female clasp together. The female lays her eggs, and at the same time the male releases his sperm. The adults usually go their separate ways afterwards, leaving the fertilized eggs to develop by themselves.

A clutch of frog eggs can look like a string of pearls, a mass of foam, or gelatin all over a pond. The trick is to keep them safe from salamanders, duck, snakes and fish, which all eat frog eggs. Many eggs don't make it. Step by step, unpromising-looking frog eggs turn into squirmy tadpoles.

Whether it's a lake or a mud puddle, most tadpoles need water. But the road to adulthood isn't the same for every species. A tadpole's diet is very simple. Most scrape algae and bacteria from underwater rocks or plants. Some eat live animals, scavenge dead ones or even eat frog eggs. And some don't need to eat at all.

First the back legs start growing, then the front. Next the mouth changes from scraping algae to swallowing whole animals. The tail shrinks, and finally lungs replace gills. The whole process can take from two weeks to three years.

Scallops in Wine Sauce

2 tablespoons olive oil
24 small bay scallops
8 to 10 mushrooms, sliced
4 green onions, chopped
2 cloves garlic, minced

2 cups purchased marinara sauce
2 tablespoons dry sherry
2 tablespoons dry white wine
4 ounces spaghetti, cooked in boiling salted
    water until al dente then drained

In a large skillet, heat olive oil over medium heat. Add scallops, mushrooms, green onions, and garlic and sauté until vegetables are tender. Add sherry, wine and marinara sauce and simmer about 3 minutes, or until scallops are tender. Serve over spaghetti. Serves 2.

Keith Ray, Chef
Spadas "Bistro" At Gold Beach

Gardens of the Sea

A weed by any other name

Most of the plants you call seaweeds are actually large marine algae. They contain chlorophyll like land plants but don't have woody stems. Seaweeds include red, green and brown algae. Two flowering plants, eelgrass and surfgrass, also grow in salt water.

Seaweeds attach themselves to rocks and other objects. They may anchor themselves 100 feet or more below the surface—as far down as they can go and still get enough light to grow. Many species live on wave-battered coasts. Others prefer quiet bays or lagoons.

It's not easy being green

Green algae are more closely related to land plants than any other marine algae. They share the same type of chlorophyll, method of food storage, and cell structure. Most green algae live between the high intertidal zone and shallow offshore waters.

One type of green algae, *Ulva*, grows in bright green sheets from floats or on rocks covered by tides twice a day. Called sea lettuce, *Ulva* has been used in salads, soups and other dishes. Coastal farmers have long used it as fertilizer and animal feed.

Some grasses are all wet

Eelgrass and surfgrass are closely related to freshwater pond weeds. They grow submerged in salt or brackish water where they flower and pollinate like most land plants. Strong root systems anchor them against surge and tides.

Eelgrass and surfgrass form underwater meadows providing shelter and food for many animals. Eelgrass prefers calm waters in protected bays where it traps sediments and is eaten by birds. Surfgrass thrives on more exposed rocks near and below the tide line.

Cioppino D'Oro

This is a stunningly gorgeous dish!

1 cup dry white wine
1/8 teaspoon saffron
2 teaspoons olive oil
1 tablespoon chopped anchovies
1/8 teaspoon salt
1/4 teaspoon freshly ground black pepper
1/8 teaspoon dried hot red chile flakes
2 teaspoons minced garlic
12 large fresh basil leaves, sliced into
   1/2-inch strips
1/2 cup chopped Roma tomatoes
16 steamer clams, scrubbed

12 mussels, scrubbed and debearded
6 ounces salmon, cut into 1-inch cubes
4 ounces halibut OR red snapper, cut into
   1-inch cubes
4 prawns, shelled and butterflied
2 ounces bay scallops
2 ounces bay shrimp
2 ounces calamari (squid), poached in water
   for 3 minutes until tender (optional)
Saffron Couscous (recipe follows)
Chopped basil for garnish

Crumble saffron into wine and set aside for 20 minutes.

In a large pot, heat olive oil over medium-high heat. Add anchovies, salt, and pepper and sauté quickly until anchovies are golden, take care not to burn them. Add dried chiles, garlic, basil, tomato, and wine and saffron in that order. Place clams and mussels in broth, cover and simmer until shells open. Remove shell fish and set aside. Add salmon, halibut, prawns, and scallops and simmer just until cooked through. Just before fish is cooked through add bay shrimp and calamari to heat through.

Place saffron couscous in a large bowl and place seafood on top. Pour broth over seafood and couscous. Garnish with chopped basil and serve immediately.

Saffron Couscous

1/2 cup chicken stock
1/8 teaspoon saffron
1/2 cup couscous
1/2 teaspoon olive oil

In a medium sauce pan, crumble saffron into chicken stock and let stand for 30 minutes.

Heat chicken stock and saffron to boiling, take pan off heat, and stir in couscous with a fork. Cover sauce pan and let sit 5 minutes. Stir olive oil into couscous, breaking up any lumps, until grains are separated and well coated. Set aside and keep warm.

Lydia Bugatti and John Cress
Bugatti's Ristorante

Yellow Eye Rock Fish

Coated in Polenta and Cracked Wheat on Basil Chive Linguini with Roasted Bacon and Shiitake Mushrooms

1 tablespoon butter	2 (5-ounce) yellow eye rock fish filets
1 clove garlic, minced	3 tablespoons olive oil
1 shallot, minced	1/2 teaspoon black pepper
1 teaspoon cracked black pepper	1/2 teaspoon salt
2 bay leaves	1/8 teaspoon cayenne pepper
1 tablespoon champagne vinegar	1/4 cup cornmeal
1/4 cup dry white wine	2 tablespoons flour
1 cup cream	2 tablespoons cracked wheat
Salt and white pepper to taste	Basil Chive Linguini (recipe follows)
5 slices bacon, chopped	Freshly grated Parmesan cheese
4 large shiitake mushrooms, julienned	Whole basil leaves

Preheat oven to 375 degrees.

In a small saucepan, melt butter over low heat. Add garlic, shallot, 1 teaspoon cracked black pepper, and bay leaves and sauté until fragrant, about 5 minutes. Raise heat to medium and add vinegar. Reduce mixture until almost dry. Add wine and reduce mixture by 1/4. Add cream and reduce by 1/4. Strain sauce and season with salt and white pepper to taste. Set aside.

Heat an oven-proof skillet over medium heat. When hot, add bacon and stir quickly to sear on all sides. Place skillet in oven and roast until bacon is crisp. Remove skillet from oven and remove bacon with a slotted spoon to paper towels to drain. Pour off fat and place skillet back on stove. Add shiitake mushrooms and sauté until tender. Remove mushrooms and add to bacon. Set aside.

Brush 1 tablespoon olive oil over yellow eye filets. Season with salt, pepper and cayenne pepper. In a shallow dish, combine corn meal, flour, and cracked wheat and stir with a fork to mix well.

Heat remaining 2 tablespoons olive oil, over medium heat, in the same skillet bacon was cooked in. Dredge fish in cornmeal mixture and place in skillet. Sear quickly on both sides. Place skillet in the oven to finish cooking, about 7 minutes.

To serve, divide linguini onto 2 plates. Place one filet on top of linguini. Sprinkle each with bacon and shiitake mushrooms. Top with sauce. Garnish with Parmesan and basil leaves. Serves 2.

Basil Chive Linguini

1 tablespoon olive oil	5 ounces linguini, cooked in boiling salted
1/2 bunch fresh basil, thinly sliced	boiling water until al dente then drained
1/2 bunch fresh chives, chopped	

In a medium skillet, heat olive oil over medium heat. Add basil, chives, and cooked linguini and sauté until fragrant, about 3 minutes. Remove from heat and set aside.

Brian Hawkins, Chef
Hotel Newport

Linguine Alla Pescatora
(Linguine, Fisherman's Style)

With thanks to Chef Paolo Biaciucci and Paola Ceccarelli in Fabriano, Italy for teaching me how to become a "real Italian chef"!

4 tablespoons olive oil
1 clove garlic, minced
1/4 teaspoon dried hot red chile flakes
1 pound rock shrimp, chopped
1 pound squid, cleaned and chopped

1 pound linguine, cooked in boiling salted water until al dente then drained
Salt to taste
Chopped fresh parsley

In a large skillet, heat olive oil over medium heat. Add garlic and red chile flakes and sauté until fragrant. Add shrimp and squid and sauté until shrimp is pink and squid is cooked. Add drained pasta to the skillet and toss with seafood. Season to taste with salt. Garnish with parsley. Serves 4 to 6.

Patricia Wied, Chef
Nature's Fresh Northwest

Below the tides

What's going on down there?

Life picks up below the low tide line. Dense stands of algae carpet the rocks, thriving in sunlit water. Many kinds of animals live here, exposed to air by only the lowest low tides. Even then they're protected by the lush seaweeds.

Shorter exposure to air means longer exposure to surging water and waves. Attaching themselves to rocks and plants secures the animals from the surge but doesn't protect them from fishes, sea stars and other predators that prowl about below.

Coastal Wetlands

Wetlands need a gentle touch

People have used coastal wetlands for centuries. We've farmed and fished them, hunted their waterfowl, dug their shellfish and built houses and harbors along their banks. Lately we've begun to appreciate the wetlands' value as hands-on ecology classrooms.

But human activity has taken its toll. Diking marshes for agriculture, filling them for development and dredging them for shipping channels alter coastal wetlands, disturbing the balance of land and water and all the plants and animals that depend on it.

What would we do without them?

Aside from their role as home for great numbers of living things, coastal wetlands help control water levels. They slow the rush of tides and absorb high water in winter. This reduces flooding and decreases the risk of erosion by fast-moving water.

Scientists are just beginning to study wetlands' role in water purification. Nutrients and pollutants settle out of water as it meanders through wetlands. Plants and other organisms feed on the nutrients and process the pollutants as well, which renders them less harmful.

When is a wetland a coastal or estuary wetland?

Wetlands are lands flooded or soaked by surface or ground water often and long enough to support plants adapted to living in wet soil. Coastal or estuary wetlands are open to the sea on one end and are influenced by saltwater tides.

Everything in its place

Coastal wetlands are a combination of several habitats connected to and bordering each other. Salt marshes of sedge, rushes and salt grass grow around nutrient-rich mudflats. Farther out, eelgrass spreads across the mud and the tidal channels beyond are full even at low tide.

For the most part, these are segregated neighborhoods. At the stream end of coastal wetlands, freshwater plants and animals thrive. At the ocean end, marine life flourishes in saltier water. In between live the plants and animals that can adjust to wetlands conditions.

Nothing stays the same

Living conditions in coastal wetlands change constantly. Daily the water in the wetlands becomes saltier with the rising tides. Seasonally, it freshens with winter rains and flooding, but turns saltier again when the rivers dry up in summer.

Seawater maintains its temperature year-round but river and wetland waters change temperature with the seasons. In summer, warm river water heats the landward side of the wetlands. But in winter, river water turns cold and the seaward side is warmer.

Coastal Wetlands

OREGON COAST AQUARIUM

*"What would the world be once bereft
of wet and of wildness? Let them be left
O let them be left, wildness and wet;
long live the weeds and the wilderness yet."*

Gerard Manley Hopkins

Coastal or estuary wetlands form at the mouths of large rivers or where streams flow into bays. As fresh river and salty tide meet and mix, the waters slow and spread out, depositing mud, sand and nutrients carried down from the forest and in from the sea.

Quiet and protected, nutrient-rich wetland waters are home to many plants and animals. They provide temporary housing for migrating birds and fishes. People, too, make use of coastal wet lands both for commercial purposes and for recreation.

Salmon

OREGON COAST
AQUARIUM

Salmon and Shrimp Cakes
with Roasted Red Pepper and Caper Mayonnaise

**2-1/2 pounds fresh salmon filet, all bones and
  skin removed**
1-1/2 pounds bay shrimp
4 cups fresh bread crumbs
1 bunch green onions, chopped
2 eggs, lightly beaten

1 teaspoon dill
1 teaspoon tarragon
1/2 teaspoon salt
Few grindings of black pepper
1 cup cracker meal OR dry bread crumbs
Olive oil

Cut the salmon into 1-inch chunks. Place in the bowl of a food processor and pulse a few times until salmon is coarsely ground. Put salmon, shrimp, bread crumbs, green onions, eggs, dill, tarragon salt, and pepper in a large bowl and mix until well blended. It is easiest to use your hands.

Form mixture into 24 patties and coat with cracker meal. Heat a non-stick sauté pan over medium heat. Add about 2 tablespoons olive oil and add patties. Cook about 5 minutes per side, or until golden. Place the cooked patties in a 200 degree oven to keep warm. Repeat until all patties are cooked. Serve with Roasted Red Pepper and Caper Mayonnaise.

Roasted Red Pepper and Caper Mayonnaise

1 red bell pepper
1 tablespoon olive oil
2 egg yolks
1 teaspoon Dijon mustard
1 teaspoon lemon juice
1/2 teaspoon salt
1/2 cup olive oil
1/2 cup vegetable oil
Few grindings black pepper
1/4 cup drained and rinsed capers
1 teaspoon tarragon

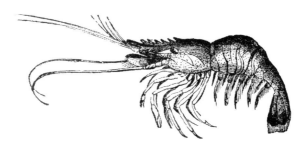

Preheat oven to 450 degrees.

To roast red pepper, cut pepper in half and discard seeds and veins. Place skin-side up on a baking sheet and brush with 1 tablespoon olive oil. Roast until charred. Remove from oven and immediately place in a bowl and cover with plastic wrap. When cool, remove and discard skin. Place in the bowl of a food processor and puree.

Place egg yolks, mustard, lemon juice, and salt in the bowl of a food processor and process to blend. Combine olive oil and vegetable oil in a measuring cup. With motor running, slowly drip oils into food processor. Mixture will become very thick. When all of the oil is incorporated, remove mayonnaise from processor and place in a mixing bowl. Stir in black pepper, capers, and tarragon. Refrigerate at least 4 hours before serving.

Kathy Goans
Tualatin Vineyards

Grilled Salmon
with Salsa Piccante

This is a wonderful sauce of parsley, pine nuts, and chopped black olives in olive oil seasoned with wine vinegar, chile pepper, and garlic. This is equally delicious over baked or poached fish.

1 cup chopped parsley
1/2 cup pine nuts
1/3 cup fresh bread crumbs
12 pitted Kalamata olives
2-1/2 tablespoons capers, rinsed and drained
4 cloves garlic
1 cup extra-virgin olive oil

2-1/2 tablespoons lemon juice
1-1/2 tablespoons sherry wine vinegar
1 teaspoon dried red chile flakes
Salt and pepper to taste

4 (6-ounce) salmon filets, skinned and all
    bones removed

Combine parsley, pine nuts, bread crumbs, olives, capers and garlic in the bowl of a food processor. Pulse until a coarse paste is formed. Add 1/3 cup of the olive oil and process until well blended. Combine remaining olive oil, lemon juice and vinegar in a measuring cup. With the motor running, add the mixture in a thin stream. Stir in chile flakes, salt, and pepper. Let sit at room temperature for 1 hour to allow flavors to marry.

Grill or broil salmon about 5 minutes per side, or until done. Serve with Salsa Piccante. Serves 4.

Catherine Whims
Genoa Restaurant

Pacific salmon
(Oncorhynchus spp.)

Pacific salmon spend most of their life at sea, but begin and end their life in fresh water. Adults navigate thousands of miles back to their native streams, where they pair off and lay bright red eggs in river-bottom gravel. The fish die soon after spawning, exhausted by their ordeal.

Chinook salmon
(Oncorhynchus tschawytscha)

Chinook, or king salmon are the largest salmon of all. They can reach 70 pounds, although 15 to 20 pounds is average. Adults spend up to five years at sea, feeding on fish, squid and shrimp.

Salmone en Agrodolce

3 pounds skinless salmon filets, all bones removed and cut into 6 to 8 portions

Marinade

2-3/4 tablespoons Dijon mustard
2-3/4 teaspoons sugar
2 tablespoons lemon juice

2 tablespoons chopped fennel greens
1-1/2 teaspoons salt
1/4 teaspoon ground fennel seeds

Whisk all marinade ingredients together in a shallow dish just large enough to hold salmon. Add salmon and toss to coat. Place a plate on salmon and weight down with a can. Cover with plastic wrap and refrigerate overnight.

Broil or grill salmon about 5 minutes per side, or until done. Serves 6 to 8.

Catherine Whims
Genoa Restaurant

Salmon Sauté
with Shiitake Mushrooms

4 tablespoons butter
2 cups sliced fresh shiitake mushrooms
3 teaspoons minced shallots
1 pound salmon filet, cut into 1-inch cubes

1 cup heavy cream
4 tablespoons sliced almonds
3 tablespoons lemon juice
Salt and pepper to taste

Melt butter in a large skillet over medium-high heat. Add shiitake mushrooms and shallots and sauté for 1 minute. Add salmon and sauté for 1 minute. Stir in cream, almonds, lemon juice, and salt and pepper to taste. Reduce heat to medium and simmer until salmon is cooked through and sauce has thickened slightly. Serve over cooked rice. Serves 4.

Justen Ruppe

Scallops

Scallops grow slowly, taking 20 years or so to mature. Outside, their shells often become encrusted with coralline algae and riddled with little holes made by boring sponges. But inside they're always beautiful: snow-white with a big purple spot by the hinge.

Steamed Salmon
Wrapped in Nori with Ginger and Garlic Marinade

Marinade (recipe follows)
4 (8-ounce) filets of salmon, skinless and
    all bones removed
2 sheets nori, sliced in half diagonally

1/4 cup diagonally sliced green onions
8 very thin slices of red bell pepper
Wasabi (Japanese horseradish)

Place salmon in the marinade and marinate 10 minutes. Remove salmon and place on a work surface. Take the half sheets of nori and wrap one around each filet.

Pour marinade and 1/4 cup additional water in the bottom of pot with a tightly fitting lid. Place a steamer rack in the pot. Place wrapped filets on the rack and cover pot. Bring to a boil then reduce heat to medium-low and steam for about 5 to 10 minutes, or until fish is cooked through. Use a spatula to transfer to individual plates. Garnish with green onions and red bell pepper slices and a dab of wasabi. Serve with steamed rice and steamed or stir-fried vegetables. Serves 4.

Marinade

    1 cup water
    1/2 cup rice wine vinegar
    1/2 cup soy sauce
    2 tablespoons grated fresh ginger
    1 tablespoon minced garlic
    1 tablespoon honey
    1/4 teaspoon dark sesame oil

Whisk marinade ingredients together in a shallow nonreactive baking dish.

Nicole M. Weiland
Umpqua Brewing Company

Salt Grilled Chinook Salmon

4 (1-inch thick) Chinook salmon steaks
3 teaspoons salt

3 tablespoons melted butter

Sprinkle salmon on both sides with salt. Place on a tray and let stand for 45 minutes.
Brush salmon with melted butter and grill over hot coals 3 to 5 minutes on each side. Salmon should be lightly browned on the outside and very moist on the inside. Serves 4.

Fae Kelly

Salmon Steaks Teriyaki

2/3 cup vegetable oil
1/2 cup soy sauce
1/4 cup sugar

2 tablespoons lemon juice
6 salmon steaks

In a shallow nonreactive dish, combine oil, soy sauce, sugar, and lemon juice and whisk until sugar dissolves. Place the salmon steaks in the marinade, cover and refrigerate at least 2 hours or overnight, turning occasionally to coat both sides.

Grill over hot coals about 5 minutes per side. Serves 6.

Nancy S. Dennis

Baby Skates

Baby skates spend as long as a year snug inside a tough, horn-like egg case. When they hatch, they're the image of their parents, only smaller, and ready to grow big on a shellfish diet.

 # *Broiled Salmon Steaks*

1/2 cup olive oil
1/4 cup light soy sauce
2 tablespoons lemon juice

1/2 teaspoon dill
1/8 teaspoon ground cloves
2 (10-ounce) salmon steaks

In a small bowl, whisk together olive oil, soy sauce, lemon juice, dill, and cloves. Brush salmon well with mixture. Broil 4 to 5 minutes per side, or until lightly browned but still moist inside. Brush with sauce during cooking. Serves 4.

Roberta Baker

Coastal Salmon Medallions

with Newport Spicy Crab Crust and Valley Vinaigrette

2 tablespoons olive oil
Salt and pepper to taste
6 (3-ounce) salmon medallions
Newport Spicy Crab Crust (recipe follows)

Valley Vinaigrette (recipe follows)
Diced red bell pepper
6 sprigs fresh tarragon

Preheat oven to 450 degrees.

Heat olive oil in a large heavy skillet over medium high heat. Season salmon with salt and pepper. Add salmon to skillet and sear briefly on both sides. Transfer salmon to a baking sheet. Divide crab mixture evenly on top of salmon. Bake until fish is cooked, about 7 to 8 minutes.

Place Vinaigrette on plates and top with salmon with crab crust. Garnish with diced red bell pepper and a sprig of fresh tarragon. Serves 6.

Newport Spicy Crab Crust

3/4 cup coconut milk
Juice of 1 orange
Zest of 1 orange, minced
Juice of 1 lime
Zest of 1 lime, minced
1 tablespoon curry paste
1-1/2 teaspoons minced garlic
1-1/2 teaspoons minced fresh ginger

2 tablespoons cornstarch
3 tablespoons cold water
1/2 cup butter, at room temperature
3/4 pound fresh crab meat
2 tablespoons diced red OR yellow bell
**   peppers**
1/2 teaspoon minced fresh tarragon

In a medium saucepan, whisk together coconut milk, orange juice, orange zest, lime juice, lime zest, curry paste, garlic, and ginger. Bring to a boil over medium-high heat and whisk until smooth. Dissolve cornstarch in water and pour into coconut milk mixture, whisking constantly. When mixture thickens, reduce heat to low and stir in butter until melted. Remove from heat and stir in crab meat, bell peppers, and tarragon. Cool.

Valley Vinaigrette

1 cucumber, peeled and chopped
2 egg yolks
3 tablespoons champagne vinegar
1 tablespoon lemon juice

1 tablespoon Dijon mustard
1/8 teaspoon sugar
Salt and pepper to taste
1 cup olive oil

Place cucumber, egg yolks, champagne vinegar, lemon juice, Dijon mustard, sugar, salt, and pepper in the bowl of a food processor and puree all together. With motor running, add the olive oil very slowly in a thin stream until all is incorporated.

Brian Hawkins, Executive Chef
Hotel Newport

Broiled Salmon Steaks
with Hazelnut Frangelico Butter

4 (8-ounce) salmon steaks
Olive oil

Salt and pepper to taste
Hazelnut Frangelico Butter (recipe follows)

Preheat broiler. Lightly oil a broiling pan.

Brush olive oil on both sides of salmon. Season with salt and pepper and place on prepared pan. Broil about 4 minutes per side, or until salmon is cooked but still moist inside. Serve with a rosette of hazelnut Frangelico butter on top of each salmon steak. Serves 4.

Hazelnut Frangelico Butter

1/2 cup butter, at room temperature
1 tablespoon Frangelico OR other hazelnut
liquor

1 tablespoon frozen orange juice concentrate
3 tablespoons chopped hazelnuts
1 tablespoon chopped parsley

Place butter in a mixing bowl and beat with an electric mixer until butter becomes pale colored. Add Frangelico and orange juice concentrate and beat until smooth. Mix in hazelnuts and parsley thoroughly. Place butter into a pastry bag fitted with a large star tip. Place a piece of plastic wrap on a plate. Pipe 4 rosettes onto the plastic wrap. Chill until firm or overnight.

Anthony Danna, Executive Chef
Kernville Katering

How small a hole is big enough for an octopus?

If the opening is big enough for the octopus's hard beak, located at the base of its head, it's big enough for the whole animal. Slipping one arm after another through the opening, the octopus twists its flexible eyeballs and pulls its body through, beak and all.

The octopus's talents run deep

The rough-skinned red octopus lurks in kelp beds or prowls sandy seafloors, hunting for snack-sized crabs. Like its larger cousin the giant Pacific octopus, the red octopus plays hard to find, easily matching the color and texture of its skin to the surroundings.

But the octopus's talents are more than skin deep. It gets a grip on life using eight muscular arms, each lined with a double row of sensitive suckers. The octopus has keen eyes connected by a complex nervous system to its well-developed brain.

Seasons of the Salmon

Pacific salmon's seasons of life

Every year, as predictable as the seasons, Pacific salmon return to spawn in the streams where they hatched. They lay eggs which develop into alevin, then fry, then fingerlings. The fingerlings become smolts and then the young salmon swim out to sea where they grow large and strong in anticipation of their journey back upstream to spawn.

Pacific salmon is not one but seven species: chinook, sockeye, chum, pink and coho salmon as well as cutthroat trout and ocean-run rainbow trout called steelhead. Each species' life cycle may differ slightly from the others, but all follow the same basic pattern: the seasons of the salmon.

At home in the gravel

Salmon eggs survive best when they're safely tucked into gravel beds and hidden from predators' view. After the eggs hatch into alevin, they continue to live in the shelter of the rocks and may actually dig themselves deeper into the gravel.

The rocky covering protects both eggs and alevin from natural hazards like freezing in winter, or being swept away by floods or being left high and dry by drought. But there is a danger of the developing fish being smothered by silt from eroding stream banks no longer stabilized by vegetation.

Salmon choose their spawning sites called redds carefully. Depending on their species, the females seek out different parts of shallow, rapidly flowing streams where the bottom is covered with gravel ranging from coarse sand to cobble-sized rocks.

Female salmon drop bright, red-orange eggs by the hundreds and thousands into pockets they've dug in the gravel of the stream bed. Once the eggs are fertilized by a male, the females bury them two to 12 inches deep as they dig yet another pocket in their redds to lay more eggs.

Eggs develop step by step

Pacific salmon eggs don't look like bait forever. After about a month, the eggs begin to show dark eyespots and they develop a vein connecting the egg yolk to what will become each fish's belly. The vein transports nutrients from the yolk to the tiny salmon and grows with the fish to meet its increasing demand for food.

In two to six months, the eyed eggs hatch into alevin, tiny translucent fish with big black eyes and spotted backs. Each alevin still has a yolk sac attached to its belly and the little fish will stay hidden in the gravel for another two to 10 weeks while they absorb the rest of the yolk's nutrients.

For Pacific salmon, the time between when the eggs are laid and when the little fish become fry is the most dangerous. In addition to natural hazards like low water and siltation, hungry cutthroat trout and other predators lurk in the streams to snap up dislodged eggs or alevin.

Like mature Pacific salmon, salmon eggs come in different sizes. Chinook salmon, the largest of the seven species, also lay the largest eggs which are about the size of a BB.

Acting their age

Fry thrive in streams that slope gently and don't flow too fast. They live in back eddies or beaver ponds, behind fallen trees or undercut tree roots. There in the slack water, they don't have to swim to stay in one place while they watch for food drifting downstream.

The fry feed on insects which have fed on algae and decaying leaves dropped into the water by streamside vegetation. As they grow, the fry move from the slow-moving edges toward the middle of the stream where there are more drifting insects to eat.

Variations in the streams

Although all Pacific salmon follow the same general life cycle, the time they spend in each stage and the part of the stream they spend it in varies. These variations occur between the seven species and also between groups of the same species in different locations.

Over the years, the salmon probably altered their behavior to make the best use of limited habitat and food supplies. Coho may spend a year or more in the streams while chum move into the estuaries as fry and pink salmon fry head straight for the sea. In this way, the salmon species don't compete with each other and increase their chance for survival.

Alevin become fry when they absorb the last of the nutrients in their yolk sacs and leave the shelter of the gravel. When they first emerge, sockeye and pink salmon fry head for the surface to gulp air into their swimbladders so they won't sink back to the stream bed.

At about an inch long, the fry are easy prey for fish like the larger salmon, sculpins and squawfish. Birds, too, like crows and kingfishers prey on salmon fry. But soon most of the fry develop vertical bands of shading down their sides called parr marks, which help camouflage the little fish in the riffles and pools where they live.

Young salmon take the scenic route

At about six inches in length, salmon fry become known as fingerlings and start the first leg of their life-long migration. They move downstream, mostly tail-first, with the oxygen-rich water flowing over their gills. By floating backwards down the stream, the fingerlings may be memorizing landmarks for the return journey.

This migration is treacherous for the young fish. To avoid predators, they often migrate at night but dead-end irrigation ditches and other manufactured hazards are more difficult to avoid. Unless dams have an overflow, fingerlings can lose direction in the slack water above them or get caught in their turbines.

Fingerlings take time to adjust

In the estuary—or before they reach it in the case of sockeye—fingerlings go through a process in which they adapt physically to their new ocean habitat. Their body chemistry changes so that the young fish, now called smolts, can survive in salt water rather than fresh.

The smolt's parr marks fade as their sides become more silvery and their backs get darker. This color pattern, called countershading, makes the fish harder to see in the open ocean. They become slimmer, more streamlined, and their tails grow longer and more deeply forked, a shape better suited for life in the Pacific.

Sockeye and pink fingerlings merely pass through estuaries on their way out to sea but chinook, chum and coho may linger as long as two months. There they grow large on the invertebrates and fish larvae they find in eelgrass beds and along the edges of the salt marsh.

Coming of age in the ocean

Pacific salmon leave their home streams to mature in the ocean. Most move to the north and northwest as they enter the salt water and then travel in a broad circular pattern around the eastern Pacific. Chum, pink and sockeye hug the coast in large schools but coho, chinook and steelhead spread out more and move farther west.

While at sea, salmon prey on plankton, squid and fishes like sand lance, herring, other salmon and rockfishes. At the same time, they must avoid predators of their own including humpback whales, orcas, northern fur seals, harbor seals, Pacific halibut, Pacific white-sided dolphins and humans.

Out to the sea and back again

After thousands of miles and as many as four years, the salmon turn south and east toward the streams where they hatched. Although scientists aren't sure, they think the earth's magnetic fields or ocean currents may guide the salmon to the general vicinity of their home streams.

Once in the area, Pacific salmon probably recognize their home streams by smell. Each stream has a unique 'odor' from the combination of chemicals washed in from the surrounding soil and deposited by streamside vegetation. Often the salmon make short trial runs up several streams before they find the right one.

Salmon make an incredible journey

Adult salmon pause only briefly in the estuaries at the mouths of their home streams. As soon as their bodies readjust to living in fresh water, the fishes begin their migration upstream to the spawning grounds.

The salmon stop eating at this time, although some will snap at a fishing lure. Instead, they use protein and fat reserves they built up in the ocean to fuel their upstream migration and production of their sperm and eggs. Sockeye may use as much as 96 percent of their fat reserves and 53 percent of their protein reserves.

Against the flow

Adult salmon migrate great distances at remarkable speeds. Chinook may go 600 miles upstream at an average speed of 52 miles per day running the gauntlet of bears, gulls, eagles and other predators, while fighting the downstream current the entire way.

The fishes also gain altitude as they migrate from sea level to spawning grounds. In the Columbia River, sockeye climb 1,500 feet, one leap at a time. The salmon are able to jump up waterfalls but must rely on fish ladders to get past dams.

Adult salmon lay in enough fat and protein reserves according to the length of their migration—the further upstream they spawn, the more reserves they need. But salmon slowed by dams, low water levels or other obstructions may use up their reserves before they ever reach the spawning grounds.

Same salmon, different look

As they begin the long journey upstream to spawn, adult salmon go through physical changes. Most change color from dark back and silvery sides to shades of green, red and black. The color patterns, which differ by species, may help the salmon recognize others of their kind at spawning time.

The fishes' muscles soften, their skin gets thicker and they absorb their scales. Males' jaws grow long and hooked, and in some species, their teeth become enlarged. Male sockeye, pink and chum salmon develop a hump which may make them easier to catch to ensure that egg-bearing females escape predators.

Grounds for reproduction

When adults reach the spawning grounds, females search out egg-laying territories called redds which they defend from other females. The best spawning grounds are gravel-bottomed shallows in clean, swiftly flowing streams where the water carries oxygen both to the spawning adults and their offspring.

The number of eggs and the size of the redd vary depending on the size of each species. Cutthroat trout, the smallest of the Pacific salmon, lay an average of 2,700 eggs in three-foot-square redds. On the other hand, chinook, the largest species, lay an average of 7,000 eggs and may require 160 square feet for their redds.

Salmon pocket their eggs

Turning on her side and slapping the gravel with her tail, a female salmon creates and pocket or hole in the stream bed. While she's digging, a male swims above her, quivering and moving from one side to the other over her tail. Soon the female lays bright red-orange eggs that sink into the gravel pocket as the male fertilizes them.

The female then moves upstream to dig another gravel pocket and another and another, as many as seven, in the same redd. Each time, the gravel she displaces washes downstream to cover the eggs she's just laid. It may take a female several days to finish spawning and her eggs may be fertilized by several males.

The cycle doesn't end

Spawning can last several days. After depositing their eggs, females live less than three weeks. Males sometimes live longer, waiting to fertilize eggs from late-arriving females. Only some of the cutthroat trout and steelhead live to spawn again another year.

All the rest of the salmon die and are eaten by scavengers like bears, crows, eagles, ravens and gulls, or decompose, returning the nutrients they gathered in the ocean to the stream providing food for the young salmon when they hatch.

Salmon Scampi

1/4 cup butter
4 large cloves garlic, minced
2 artichoke hearts, quartered
1/2 cup sliced mushrooms
1 stalk celery, finely chopped
1/4 cup chopped red onion
2 tablespoons minced parsley
1/4 cup chopped tomato
1/4 cup dry white wine

1/4 teaspoon celery seed
1/4 teaspoon lemon juice
1/4 teaspoon Tabasco sauce
1/4 teaspoon Worcestershire sauce
1/4 teaspoon salt
1/4 teaspoon white pepper
2 (4 to 6-ounce) salmon filets, boneless and
   skinless

In large sauté pan, melt the butter over medium heat. Add garlic, artichoke hearts, mushrooms, celery, onions, and parsley and sauté until fragrant, about 2 to 4 minutes. Add tomato and wine and simmer 2 minutes. Stir in celery seed, lemon juice, Tabasco sauce, Worcestershire sauce, salt, and white pepper and simmer 1 minute. Add salmon and simmer for about 4 minutes on each side, or until cooked through but still moist inside. Serve over rice. Serves 4.

Kathy Sallander
Flying Gull Restaurant

Salmon à la Baltimore

4 (4-ounce) salmon steaks
1 tablespoon lemon juice
1 tablespoon lite soy sauce
2 teaspoons minced fresh dill

2 teaspoons minced garlic
2 teaspoons Old Bay Seasoning
1/8 teaspoon white pepper
Lemon wedges

Preheat oven to 375 degrees. Coat a 9-inch by 13-inch baking dish with vegetable spray.

Place salmon in prepared baking dish. Sprinkle lemon juice and soy sauce over steaks. Then sprinkle over dill, garlic, Old Bay Seasoning and white pepper. Cover with foil. Bake for 8 to 10 minutes or until salmon is cooked through. Garnish with lemon wedges. Serves 4.

Marilyn D. Switzer, Executive Chef
Greenleaf Restaurant

Pesto Crusted Salmon

with Wild Mushroom Risotto and Grilled Red Onion and Pepper Slaw

2 (6-ounce) salmon filets
Pesto Crust (recipe follows)
2 tablespoons olive oil

Grilled Red Onion and Pepper Slaw
 (recipe follows)
Wild Mushroom Risotto (recipe follows)

Dredge salmon filets in Pesto Crust until well coated on both sides. Heat olive oil in a large cast iron skillet over medium-high heat. Place salmon in skillet and cook about 4 minutes per side, or until cooked through but still moist inside. Divide Wild Mushroom Risotto onto 2 plates. Divide Grilled Onion and Pepper Slaw next to risotto. Place a salmon filet on top of risotto. Serve immediately. Serves 2.

Pesto Crust

1/4 cup pine nuts, lightly toasted
1/2 cup dry bread crumbs
1/2 cup packed basil leaves
1/4 cup flour

1/4 cup freshly grated Parmesan cheese
4 cloves garlic, minced
Salt and pepper to taste

To toast pine nuts, place on a baking sheet and toast in a 350 degree oven for about 10 minutes, or until golden. Cool. Place all ingredients in the bowl of a food processor and process until smooth.

Grilled Red Onion and Pepper Slaw

1/4 cup balsamic vinegar
1/2 teaspoon minced garlic
1/2 teaspoon minced fresh thyme
Freshly ground black pepper to taste

1/3 cup olive oil
2 red onions, thickly sliced
1 red bell pepper, thickly sliced
1 yellow bell pepper, thickly sliced

In a medium bowl, whisk together vinegar, garlic, thyme, and pepper. Add olive oil in a thin stream, whisking constantly, until all oil is incorporated. Grill onions and peppers until tender. Add to the vinaigrette and toss well. Cover and chill 2 hours before serving.

Wild Mushroom Risotto

1 tablespoon butter
1 tablespoon minced garlic
1 cup sliced wild mushrooms
1 cup Arborio rice

2 cups chicken stock
1/2 cup Chianti OR other dry red wine
1/2 cup freshly grated Parmesan

In a medium saucepan, melt butter over medium heat. Add garlic and mushrooms and sauté until tender. Add rice and stir until well coated with butter. In a small sauce pan, combine chicken stock and wine and bring to a boil. Slowly stir in hot stock to the rice, stirring constantly. Simmer over medium heat, stirring often, until liquid is absorbed, about 15 minutes. Stir in Parmesan and serve immediately.

Mick Hug, Executive Chef
Kah Nee Ta Resort

Coastal Wetland Birds

Mudflats give food to the flocks

The mudflats appear as the tide falls. Flocks of hungry shorebirds follow the receding water, probing in the sticky mud with their sharp beaks. There's plenty for dowitchers, sandpipers, curlews and all. Each bird eats animals buried as deep as its beak is long.

High tide and the pickings are easy for wading birds like great blue herons and divers like scoters and cormorants. They feed well on fish, crabs and other invertebrates that come to the mudflats in search of snails, shrimp and worms.

Eelgrass feeds birds on the go

Lush beds of eelgrass play host to birds all year long. Herons stalk fish and shrimp year-round. In spring and fall, migrating ducks, geese and swans stop for a quick bite to eat before moving on.

Some waterfowl stay the winter, making the most of all the eelgrass has to offer. Black brant and Canada geese eat the entire eelgrass plant. Northern pintails prefer just the seeds while bufflehead search the blades for shrimp and snails.

Salt marshes are shelters for all

No matter what the season, salt marshes are for the birds. Dense marsh grasses shelter songsparrow and marsh wren nests in summer. Swallows flit overhead chasing insects, while crows scavenge for leftovers, keeping the marsh clean.

Fall and spring find the salt marsh full of migrating waterfowl that stop to rest and feed. Canada geese and a number of ducks spend the winter in Oregon marshes feeding on the ample supply of grass seeds and shoots.

Birds eat channel rations

Birds make good use of both the tidal channels and their shallow edges. Greges, cormorants and waterfowl feed on the surface of the channels or dive for plants and animals along the bottom. Kingfishers and bald eagles fly overhead, swooping down to catch fish.

Wading birds like the great blue heron stroll through the shallows stirring up small fish with their feet. At high tide, dowitchers and other shorebirds probe the channel banks for clams and shrimp buried in the mud.

Salmon Loaf

1 cup finely chopped celery
1 cup finely chopped onion
1/2 cup cream
2 eggs, beaten
2 tablespoons Worcestershire sauce
1 tablespoon minced fresh parsley
1 teaspoon paprika

1/2 teaspoon salt
1/2 teaspoon pepper
1 pound cooked salmon OR
    1 (14-1/2-ounce) can salmon, flaked
2 cups fresh breadcrumbs
2 tablespoons melted butter

Preheat oven to 400 degrees. Lightly oil a loaf pan.

In a large bowl, mix together celery, onion, cream, eggs, Worcestershire sauce, parsley, paprika, salt, and pepper and blend well. Add salmon and breadcrumbs and mix well. Place mixture in prepared loaf pan and pour melted butter over the top. Bake for about 35 minutes or until golden brown.

Stewart Whipple

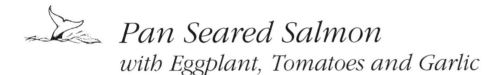

Pan Seared Salmon
with Eggplant, Tomatoes and Garlic

4 (6-ounce) salmon filets, boneless and skinless
Salt and freshly ground pepper
2 tablespoons olive oil
1-1/4 cup (1/2-inch) diced eggplant
3/4 cup chopped tomatoes

10 cloves garlic, minced
2 tablespoons dry white wine
1 tablespoon lemon juice
Chopped fresh parsley
Lemon wedges

Generously season salmon with salt and pepper. In a large skillet, heat olive oil over medium heat. Place salmon in preheated skillet and sear 3 to 4 minutes on each side. Remove to a serving platter and keep warm.

Add eggplant, tomatoes, and garlic and sauté until eggplant is tender. Add wine and lemon juice and sauté until liquid is absorbed. Pour vegetable mixture over salmon. Garnish with parsley and lemon wedges. Serves 4.

Thomas J. Smith, Executive Chef
Oregon Electric Station Restaurant
and Lounge

Pan Seared Chinook Salmon

with Hazelnut Crust on Celery Root Puree and Oregon Mushroom-Leek Ragout

4 (6-ounce) Chinook salmon filets
Salt and pepper
1 cup ground Oregon hazelnuts
2 tablespoons olive oil

Celery Root Puree (recipe follows)
Oregon Mushroom-Leek Ragout
(recipe follows)
4 fresh rosemary sprigs

Preheat oven to 400 degrees.

Lightly season salmon with salt and pepper. Place bone side of each filet in hazelnuts and press gently. Heat olive oil in a large sauté pan over medium heat. Add salmon, nut side down, to pan. Sear for 2 to 3 minutes, or until nuts are lightly brown. Remove filets from sauté pan and place nut side up on a baking sheet. Bake for about 5 minutes or until just cooked through.

Divide Celery Root Puree evenly in the middle of 4 plates. Spoon Mushroom Ragout around puree and place salmon on top of Celery Root Puree. Garnish with a rosemary sprig. Serves 4.

Celery Root Puree

3 to 4 pounds celery root
2 medium potatoes
1/4 cup butter, at room temperature

1/4 cup buttermilk
1 teaspoon salt

Trim off ends of celery root. Lay on flat end and, using a sharp knife, trim off the skin following the contour of the bulb. Cut into 2-inch cubes. Peel the potatoes and cut into 2-inch cubes. Place in a pot and cover with water. Bring to a boil and simmer for 6 to 8 minutes, or until tender. Drain well. Transfer to a mixing bowl. Add butter, buttermilk, and salt and mash until smooth. Keep warm until ready to serve.

Oregon Mushroom-Leek Ragout

3 tablespoons butter
1 tablespoon olive oil
12 ounces sliced Oregon mushrooms such as
**   chanterelle, shiitake, oyster or any**
**   combination of what is available**
1 teaspoon minced garlic

1/2 cup dry white wine
2 cups clam juice OR chicken stock
2 leeks (white and pale green part only),
**   cleaned well and julienned**
1 teaspoon minced fresh rosemary
Salt and pepper to taste

In a large sauté pan, melt 1 tablespoon of the butter and olive oil together over medium heat. Add mushrooms and sauté for about 2 minutes. Add garlic and sauté an additional 2 minutes. Add the wine and reduce by one third. Add clam juice and bring to a boil over high heat. Add leeks and rosemary. Reduce by one third and remove from heat. Stir in the remaining butter. Season to taste with salt and pepper. Keep warm until ready to serve.

Greg Meixner, Executive Chef
Leslie and Dennis Dressel, Proprietors
Bay House Restaurant

Cool Salmon Steaks and Vegetables
with Radish Tartar Sauce

1 pound green beans
4 (6 to 8-ounce) salmon steaks
8 to 12 red new potatoes
4 butter lettuce leaves

1-1/2 cups cherry tomatoes
Radish Tartar Sauce (recipe follows)
Lemon wedges

In a large pot, bring 3 quarts of water to a boil over high heat. Add beans and blanch until they are bright green and barely tender. Remove beans with tongs and plunge into ice water to cool. Drain well and chill.

Return water to a boil and add salmon. Cover pot tightly and remove from heat. Let stand until fish is cooked, about 14 minutes. Remove fish carefully and place in ice water to cool. Drain well and chill.

Return water to a boil and add potatoes. When water comes to a boil, reduce heat to medium, cover pot, and simmer until potatoes are tender when pierced, about 20 minutes. Remove potatoes and plunge into ice water. Drain well and chill.

On a large serving platter, lay lettuce leaves on one end. Top with the poached salmon steaks. Place the beans, potatoes and tomatoes alongside the fish, grouping each separately. Serve with radish tartar sauce and lemon wedges. Serves 4.

Radish Tartar Sauce

1 cup sour cream OR plain yogurt
3/4 cup chopped red radish
1/3 cup finely chopped green onion

2 tablespoons drained capers
1 tablespoon prepared horseradish
Salt to taste

In a medium bowl, combine all ingredients and blend well. Chill at least 3 hours before serving to allow flavors to develop.

Roberta Baker

Bat ray (*Myliobatis californica*)

Bat rays have flattened bodies and wing-like fins. These shark relatives cruise the bottom of sandy or muddy bays, flapping their fins. Sometimes they stir up the sand with their fins to uncover the clams, oysters and snails they eat.

Bat rays are especially equipped to live on the bottom of muddy bays or sandy seafloors. They breathe through modified gill openings called spiracles on top of their heads and suck food from the mud with mouths on the bottom of their heads.

Bat ray bodies are designed for bottom-living. They're flattened from back to belly with broad, wing-like pectoral fins. These rays glide over the seafloor in search of food or settle down, flapping a concealing layer of sand over themselves with their fins.

Broiled Salmon Steaks
with Dill Butter

2 tablespoons dry white wine
1 tablespoon minced shallots
1 tablespoon olive oil
1/2 teaspoon grated lemon zest
1/4 teaspoon thyme

6 (1-inch thick) salmon steaks
2 tablespoons melted butter
Salt and pepper
Dill Butter (recipe follows)

In a shallow dish, whisk together wine, shallots, olive oil, lemon zest, and thyme. Place salmon steaks in dish and marinate for 1 hour, turning once.

Place marinated salmon steaks on a broiling pan and brush with melted butter. Season with salt and pepper and broil 5 minutes on each side. Serve with Dill Butter. Serves 6.

Dill Butter

1/2 cup butter, at room temperature
2 tablespoons lemon juice
1 tablespoon dill

2 drops Tabasco sauce
Salt and pepper to taste

Combine all ingredients in a small bowl and blend well. Refrigerate until firm before serving.

Fae Kelly

Sharks have gotten a bad rap

Sharks haven't changed much in the last 100 million years. Torpedo-shaped to glide through the sea, these hunters are armed with tough sandpapery skin, a keen nose and an endless supply of teeth to replace lost or worn ones.

Despite popular myth, sharks are not vicious, bloodthirsty killers that devour anything they can sink their teeth into. Like wolves, they usually hunt sick or injured animals, and most sharks attack humans only when they mistake them for food.

What does a 40-foot-long shark eat?

Anything it wants? No. The whale shark—the world's largest fish—has tiny, useless teeth. It uses strainer-like gill rakers instead to filter food from the water, and though its mouth is six feet wide, it never eats anything bigger than plankton and little fish.

Salmon with a Spicy Honey-Lavender Glaze

4 tablespoons honey
1 tablespoon minced lavender blossoms
1 tablespoon white vinegar
1 tablespoon water

1 teaspoon cayenne pepper
1/2 teaspoon minced garlic
Salt to taste
2 pounds salmon filets

Prepare grill.

In a small bowl, mix together honey, lavender, vinegar, water, cayenne, garlic, and salt. Liberally brush mixture over salmon. Grill salmon about 5 minutes per side, or until cooked through but still moist inside. Brush salmon with glaze throughout grilling.

Victor Chamorro, Executive Chef
Nature's Fresh Northwest

Invisible Barriers

From the surface, the ocean appears to be one vast expanse of water stretching to the horizon. But to the organisms that live there, the ocean consists of distinct zones separated by invisible but very real boundaries. Plants are confined to the sunlit upper layers of the sea. They and the animals that eat them flourish in the nutrient-rich zone where cold water wells up from the deep. All sea life is influenced by changes in the salinity and temperature of its surroundings.

Temperature, salinity, and density work together to affect sea life. Cold water holds more oxygen than warm water so organisms like salmon that need plenty of oxygen do well in colder water. Cold water is denser, too, and carries oxygen to life on the seafloor when it sinks.

Rain and runoff from rivers affect the salinity of seawater. Life in the surface waters must adjust to these seasonal changes. But salty water, like cold water, is dense and sinks below fresh water, so deep water animals can rely on a steady supply of salty water.

For about 100 feet, enough light filters through seawater for plants to grow. This photic zone produces the plankton which support the ocean food web. Here, in the upper 10 percent of the sea, is where all the plant growth occurs. In the other 90 percent of the ocean, the aphotic zone, twilight fades to total darkness. Animals here travel upward in the night for food or survive on dead organic matter carried down from above. And some are active hunters, preying on other animals.

The northwest winds of summer push the upper layer of seawater to the south and west, away from the Oregon coast. It's replaced by cold, nutrient-rich water that wells up from depths of 300 to 600 feet and forms a cold water zone six to 18 miles wide along the shore.

With long periods of sunlight and nutrients from the deep, this upwelling zone is able to produce three times more plant plankton than the open sea. Schools of anchovy and sardines are drawn to this abundant food supply, as are predators like salmon and tuna.

Marine Mammal
Stories

Steller sea lions keep their distance

Light tan Steller sea lions, larger but more timid than California sea lions, are usually seen on offshore rocks or in secluded coves. Listed as threatened by the National Marine Fisheries Service, these sea lions breed in Oregon from May through August.

Known for its nose

During the summer, northern elephant seals often haul out at Cape Arago. These immature males look a lot like large harbor seals but without spots. If you find a molting elephant seal in an isolated cove or beach, leave it alone to shed its coat and later return to sea.

Harbor porpoises are shy

More harbor porpoises may live off the Oregon coast than any other cetacean, but you couldn't tell by looking out to sea. This dark gray porpoise rarely jumps clear of the water and only occasionally treats whale watchers to a glimpse of its triangular dorsal fin.

Thar she blows!

From December to May, look for a spout offshore. If it's followed by a mottled gray back with "knuckle bumps" but no dorsal fin, you've just seen a gray whale! They pass Oregon twice on their annual migration between the Arctic and Mexico.

Surf's up!

Large herds of sleek Pacific white-sided dolphins come close to shore in winter and spring. These acrobatic dolphins show their true colors—dark gray backs and lighter side stripes—when leaping and surfing in bow waves. They like to play in boat wakes, too!

All dressed up

Orcas are hard to miss with their dashing black-and-white colors and tall dorsal fins. They usually travel in family "pods" when they visit the Oregon coast to hunt fish, sea lions and seals. Sometimes they enter bays, seeking prey.

Marine Mammals

OREGON COAST
AQUARIUM

The Open Ocean Exhibit

The Open Ocean Exhibit is a rehabilitation facility designed especially for killer whales. The main pool measures 150 feet long, 75 feet wide and 25 feet deep, and holds two million gallons of cold, clean sea water pumped directly from Yaquina Bay. Reef-like rockwork covers half the pool's bottom, providing a rubbing surface, acoustic variety, and orca-sized canyons and crannies. Water current within the pool can be altered (clockwise, counterclockwise, scrambled), discouraging repetitive single-direction or "stereotypic" swimming. Play jets in pool bottom can create a vertical water curtain or air-bubble curtain. A separate medical pool allows for treatment if required. Two underwater viewing windows measure eight feet tall by 24 feet wide; a third measures eight feet tall by 16 feet wide. Visitors can see the killer whale, and the killer whale can see visitors.

The Seal and Sea Lion Exhibit

Seals and sea lions are mainstays of Oregon's marine mammal community. Sea lions can often be heard barking in Newport's Yaquina Bay, and harbor seals regularly ply the waters off the jetty. Both species are exhibited in the Aquarium's large outdoor pool. The exhibit allows visitors to learn about these marine mammals' natural behaviors both from animal husbandry demonstrations and from Aquarium interpreters stationed at the exhibit.

The Sea Otter Exhibit

Sea otters, extinct on the Oregon Coast since the early 1900s, have now returned to the state through the Oregon Coast Aquarium. Currently living in the Aquarium's large sea otter exhibit are three northern or Alaska sea otters: Cody, a 74-pound male; Kiana, a 63-pound female; and Sitka, a 54-pound female. All are roughly 6 years old, and were rescued during the 1989 Exxon Valdez oil spill in Prince William Sound, Alaska.

Seafood

OREGON COAST
AQUARIUM

Oven Baked Marinated Monkfish
with Sweet and Sour Sauce

4 (6 to 8-ounce) monkfish filets
2-1/2 cups sake OR other rice wine
1/4 cup sugar

2 tablespoons soy sauce
Sweet and Sour Sauce (recipe follows)

Remove any gray membrane from monkfish if necessary. Butterfly the filets to attain even thickness. Place in a 9-inch by 13-inch baking dish. Combine 2 cups sake, sugar and soy sauce and pour over fish. Refrigerate for 45 minutes.

Preheat oven to 350 degrees.

Remove monkfish from marinade and discard marinade. Return fish to baking dish and pour over remaining 1/2 cup sake. Bake for 10 to 15 minutes, taking care not to overcook fish. Remove monkfish filets to a warm platter and pour Sweet and Sour Sauce over. Serves 6.

Sweet and Sour Sauce

3 tablespoons vegetable oil
1/2 cup chopped green onions
1 teaspoon minced garlic
1 teaspoon minced fresh ginger
1 cup rice wine vinegar
1 cup sugar
3/4 cup chicken stock
7 tablespoons ketchup
1/4 cup Chinese wine OR dry sherry
2 tablespoons soy sauce
1 teaspoon Thai sweet chile sauce
Salt and white pepper to taste
1 tablespoon cornstarch
3 tablespoons cold water

In a medium saucepan, heat oil over medium heat. Add green onions, garlic and ginger and sauté until fragrant. Stir in rice wine vinegar, sugar, chicken stock, ketchup, Chinese wine, soy sauce, sweet chile sauce, salt and pepper and bring to a boil. Blend cornstarch and water together and whisk into mixture. Cook over medium-high heat, stirring constantly, until thickened.

Koji Oishi
Elizabeth's

Halibut with Beurre Blanc Sauce

2 (6-ounce) halibut steaks
1/4 cup dry white wine
2 tablespoons butter
1 clove garlic, minced

1 tablespoon chopped fresh basil
1 tablespoon chopped fresh dill
Beurre Blanc Sauce (recipe follows)

Preheat oven to 350 degrees.

Place halibut in a baking dish just large enough to hold them. Pour over wine. Dot with butter and sprinkle garlic, basil and dill on top. Bake for 15 to 25 minutes or until halibut is just cooked through. Serve topped with Beurre Blanc Sauce. A good accompaniment would be steamed red potatoes. Serves 2.

Beurre Blanc Sauce

1/4 cup dry white wine
1/4 cup heavy cream

3 tablespoons cold butter, cut into pieces

Pour wine in a small saucepan. Simmer over medium heat until reduced by half. Add cream and reduce mixture by two-thirds. Remove from heat and whisk in butter, a little at a time, until all is incorporated. Sauce will be creamy.

Chris Phillips

Halibut

Halibut's tender white flesh makes it a favorite Northwest seafood. "Longliners" catch halibut with baited hooks tied to lines that stretch for miles along the seafloor. To keep the fleet from catching too many, a special international commission regulates the halibut fishery.

Pacific halibut (Hippoglosus stenolepis)

The Pacific halibut spawns in winter in deep water. The eggs rise slowly as they develop, then surface currents carry the juveniles toward shore. By summer, the upright juveniles have flattened into adults living on their sides on the bottom. Later, they migrate back to deep water offshore.

Broiled Thresher Shark with Chilean Sauce

1 cup Cayenne pepper sauce, such as Durkees
1/2 cup purchased barbeque sauce
1 tablespoon freshly ground pepper
1 tablespoon lemon juice

2 teaspoons dried red hot chile flakes
1/2 teaspoon Tabasco sauce

6 (6-ounce) thresher shark filets

In a small bowl, whisk together Cayenne pepper sauce, barbeque sauce, pepper, lemon juice, hot chile flakes, and Tabasco sauce. Cover and refrigerate 2 hours to allow flavors to develop.

Brush filets well on both sides with sauce. Broil 5 minutes per side, or until cooked through, basting several times with sauce while cooking. Serves 6.

Thomas James Smith, Executive Chef
Oregon Electric Station Restaurant
and Lounge

 # Snapper Vera Cruz

12 ounces red snapper filets
Flour
1/4 cup olive oil
1 cup chopped red onion
1 cup julienned green bell pepper
1 cup julienned red bell pepper
2/3 cup chopped tomato

1 tablespoon chopped cilantro
1 teaspoon minced garlic
1/2 teaspoon salt
1/2 teaspoon pepper
1 tablespoon butter
1/4 cup orange juice
1/4 cup dry white wine

Lightly dust red snapper with the flour. In a large skillet, heat the olive oil over medium heat. Add snapper, onion, green and red bell peppers, tomato, cilantro, garlic, salt, and pepper and cook 3 minutes. Turn the fish and add the butter. Just when the butter starts to brown, add the orange juice and wine. Simmer for 3 minutes or until fish is cooked through. Place the red snapper on a serving plate and spoon the sauce over. Serves 2.

Colin Cox
Oregon Electric Station Restaurant
and Lounge

An Orca Primer

Killer whales live in all the world's oceans, traveling in small groups and preying on fishes and larger animals. Typical sizes for killer whales are: newborn calf: 7 to 8 feet; adult female: 17 to 24 feet; and adult male 22 to 27 feet.

With a mouthful of 40 to 48 sharp, three-inch teeth, killer whales are the top predator wherever they go; only humans hunt them. An adult killer whale consumes 100 to 300 pounds of food a day. Their diet includes a wide variety of ocean animals, especially salmon, herring and squid. The diet of some killer whales also includes seals, sea lions, walruses, sea otters, dolphins, sea birds, sea turtles and even other whales.

Two types of killer whales—residents and transients—form separate communities with different ways of life.

- Residents remain in a small home range; transients roam over a large area.
- Residents live in pods of five to 50; transients in pods of one to seven.
- Residents eat fishes and squid; transients prey on marine mammals such as seals, sea lions and other whales.
- Residents make sounds often, and have repertoires of five to 15 calls; transients call less often, and have three to four calls.
- Transients stay underwater longer, sometimes for more than 10 minutes.
- Residents and transient killer whales populations have been most extensively studied in Puget Sound. Whales elsewhere may live differently.

The orcas in a pod communicate with each other using several different calls. We humans don't know just what each call means, but orcas communicate when they're separated, when they meet another pod or when deciding where to go or what to do next. A pod's group of sounds is called a dialect. Even though pods regularly meet and mingle, each keeps its own unique dialect. However, dialects do change over time—very slowly.

Orcas find prey and navigate by sending clicks and buzzes out into the dark, murky water and listening for the echo to bounce back. Sound travels about five times faster through water than air, so it's a quick way to determine what's out there.

Cows may give birth as often as every three years, but may wait as long as eight years. Following a 16 to 17 month gestation period, an eight-foot-long calf is born, often helped to the surface by a female pod-mate.

- For the first six months, a calf stays close to its mother using her slipstream for easier swimming. It nurses a few seconds at a time, several times an hour, around the clock. It is weaned at about one year of age.

- Until they are about six, calves spend much time playing—chasing and splashing each other. From the age of seven on, females spend more time looking after younger whales, and adolescent males spend more time alone or hanging out with the mature bulls.

- Orca bulls are ready to mate (often with females outside their pod) at 10 to 13 years of age. Cows are ready at 9 to 10 and give birth to their first calf between the ages of 11 and 17.

- Orcas live between 25 and 40 years; recent studies suggest they might live even longer. Only four percent of the adult pod members die each year, but orcas reproduce slowly because nearly half of the calves born die before they reach one year of age.

Killer whales live in groups called pods. A pod is made up of related whales of both sexes and all ages, and usually has from five to 30 members. The group travels together, hunts cooperatively and takes care of its members.

- Sometimes two or more pods may join up into a herd of 50 to 100 whales. The herd will stay together for a while, hunting and traveling, and then break up into the very same pods as before.

- A mature female killer whale is the dominant whale in the pod. She gets and stays that way through a variety of behaviors—ramming and biting other whales, snapping or popping her jaws, and splashing with her flukes or flippers.

Sometimes a pod of killer whales will work together to encircle and herd fish into a small area for easy feeding. Those that eat animals such as seals and penguins have their own methods: surfacing under ice floes to tip the ice and throw prey into the water; using their tail flukes to send a wall of water over the ice floe and wash prey into the water; chasing seals and sea lions and hitting them with their tails, sometimes for more than an hour; and when attacking baleen whales, biting off chunks of flesh or blubber, or grasping the prey by the flukes or flippers to slow its escape.

As it swims along near the water's surface, an orca comes up every 30 seconds or so to breathe. These whales most often cruise at two to six miles an hour, though they have been clocked at 30 miles an hour.

- To hunt for fish, an orca frequently dives down to 100 or 200 feet deep for an average of four or five minutes. If they need to, orcas can dive to almost 1000 feet for more than 10 minutes.

- Pound for pound, whales don't have any bigger lungs than land mammals. In fact, the deepest-diving species have the smallest lungs. And to top it off, whales breathe slower. The difference is that they breathe deeper and extract more oxygen.

- Whale blood can carry a huge oxygen load. It's chock-full of red blood cells with concentrated oxygen-carrying hemoglobin. Toothed whales, like the killer whale, store oxygen in their muscles, too, in a substance called myoglobin.

- A whale's heart rate slows as it dives, using less oxygen. Blood is shunted away from parts that need less oxygen and concentrated toward the heart, lungs and brain, which all need a good oxygen supply.

Black Sesame Seed Crusted Ahi
with Wasabi and Pickled Ginger

Ahi Marinade (recipe follows)
4 (6-ounce) ahi tuna steaks
1 cup black sesame seeds
3 tablespoons dark sesame oil

2 tablespoons wasabi
1 tablespoon water
4 tablespoons pickled ginger
4 lemon wedges

Place ahi tuna in marinade and let stand for 20 minutes, turning occasionally.

Place sesame seeds on a flat plate. Remove ahi from marinade and press into seeds on both sides making sure that fish is completely coated. In a large skillet, heat sesame oil over medium heat. Add sesame crusted ahi steaks and cook for 3 to 4 minutes. Turn and cook an additional 5 minutes, or until fish is cooked through.

Blend wasabi powder with water to make a thick paste, then divide into 4 portions and roll into balls. Place Ahi steaks on plates and top with 1 ball of wasabi, a lemon wedge and 1 tablespoon pickled ginger. Serves 4.

Ahi Marinade

1/2 cup soy sauce
1/4 cup dry sherry
1/4 cup grated fresh ginger

2 tablespoons rice wine vinegar
1 tablespoon dark sesame oil
1/8 teaspoon black pepper

Combine all ingredients in a shallow dish and whisk until well blended.

Andrew Mueller, Chez Jeannette

Whales of the Oregon Coast

Whales, dolphins and porpoises are marine mammals called cetaceans. Like land mammals, cetaceans are warm-blooded and breathe air. They bear and nurse live young and, although you can't see it, all cetaceans have hair at some time in their lives.

There are two types of cetaceans: toothed whales like orcas and dolphins, and baleen whales like gray and humpback whales. Toothed whales hunt fish, squid and sometimes other marine mammals. Baleen whales sift seawater for small fish and shrimp-like krill.

Those bumps are barnacles that live on gray whales and nowhere else. The barnacles anchor themselves in the whale's blubber, hitching a ride to nutrient-rich waters where they strain food from the sea. It's a good deal, but when the whale dies and washes ashore, its barnacles die, too.

Despite their size, whales move with surprising grace and speed. Powerful tails and wide flukes propel their streamlined bodies. Flippers help whales steer and balance. A dorsal fin acts as a stabilizer on some smaller whales.

Whales breathe through blowholes on top of their heads. Toothed whales have one opening in their blowholes, baleen whales have two. Whales don't spout water—they exhale water vapor that condenses in the air.

Cabazon
with Crawfish and Chipotle Salsa

Cabazon is a member of the green ling family which also includes ling cod. This family of fish got their name because of the occasional light green color of the raw meat. All of the meat is white after being fully cooked. Cabazon is a firm textured fish which makes it excellent for grilling.

2 tablespoons olive oil	**Juice of 1/2 lime**
2 cups lightly packed fresh basil, chopped	**1 teaspoon canned chipotle chile, minced**
1/3 cup chopped tomatoes	**1/2 teaspoon cumin**
1 teaspoon minced garlic	**2 (8-ounce) cabazon filets**
4 ounces crawfish tail meat	**Olive oil**
1/4 cup dry sherry	**Salt and pepper**

In a large skillet, heat olive oil over medium-high heat. Add basil, tomatoes, garlic, and crawfish and sauté quickly for 2 minutes. Add sherry and simmer for 3 minutes. Add lime juice, chipotle chile, and cumin and heat through. Remove from heat and keep warm.

Prepare barbeque. Lightly brush cabazon filets with olive oil and season with salt and pepper. Grill over medium-hot coals until cooked through, about 4 minutes on each side. Place cabazon on serving plate and cover with crawfish and chipotle salsa leaving fish exposed on both ends. Serves 2.

Meryln Baker
Jake's Famous Crawfish Restaurant

Whales rely in part on their size to help them stay warm: large bodies hold heat better than small ones. Thick blubber insulates them, and they heat cold blood flowing in from fins and flukes with warm blood flowing out from the heart.

Baleen whales gulp a huge mouthful of food and water, then squirt the water out through baleen plates with their tongues. The fringed baleen acts like a sieve, trapping food inside the whale's mouth.

Some toothed whales use echolocation, a sort of sonar, to navigate and find prey. The whales send out sound waves which bounce off unseen objects. Returning echoes tell whales how far away the objects are and give them a clue about their shape.

Many baleen whales follow annual migration routes through the eastern Pacific Ocean. They spend the summer in cold, northern waters where food is plentiful. The whales move south in winter to warmer waters where they breed and give birth to their calves.

Some, like the gray whale, hug the coast when they migrate. Their routes are well-known and frequently studied. Open sea migration routes are harder to follow and scientists don't know where some species go when they head out to sea. Baleen whales migrate farther than most toothed whales. The gray whale holds the record for the longest migration of any mammal. It travels 12,000 miles each year on its round trip between feeding grounds off Alaska and breeding grounds off Baja California.

Red Snapper
with Goat Cheese and Peppercorns

1 teaspoon whole black peppercorns
1 teaspoon whole dry green peppercorns
1 teaspoon whole red peppercorns
1 teaspoon whole white peppercorns
1 teaspoon dried hot red chile flakes
1/2 teaspoon salt

5 ounces soft goat cheese such as Montrachet
3 tablespoons sour cream
5 cloves garlic, minced
1/2 cup heavy cream
2 pounds red snapper fillets
2 tablespoons melted butter

Preheat oven to 400 degrees. Lightly oil a shallow baking dish large enough to hold fish in a single layer.

Place all peppercorns, dried chiles, and salt in a spice grinder or a coffee grinder and grind medium coarse. Place peppercorn mixture, goat cheese, sour cream, and garlic in the bowl of a food processor. Pulse until well combined. With motor running, add the cream slowly just until mixture is smooth.

Place red snapper in prepared baking dish. Rub melted butter over fish. Spread the goat cheese mixture evenly over red snapper. Bake until just cooked through, about 15 minutes. Turn on broiler and broil just until a few brown spots appear, about 2 minutes. Serves 6.

Winterborne Restaurant

 # Yellowfin Tuna
with Blackberry Vinaigrette

1 egg yolk
1 cup olive oil
1 cup sweet rice wine
1/2 cup red wine vinegar

1 pound blackberries, pureed
Salt and pepper
4 4-ounce yellowfin tuna steaks
4 cups mixed fresh greens

Place egg yolk in a medium bowl. Whisking constantly, add olive oil a few drops at a time until mixture is thick and emulsified. Slowly whisk in the sweet rice wine and the vinegar. Stir in 1/2 cup of the blackberry puree and season with salt and pepper. Set aside.

Rub the tuna steaks with the remaining blackberry puree. Broil until medium-rare, about 4 minutes per side.

Place greens on 4 plates. Top with broiled tuna steaks and pour blackberry vinaigrette over. Serves 4.

John Gorham, Sous Chef
Oregon Electric Station Restaurant
and Lounge

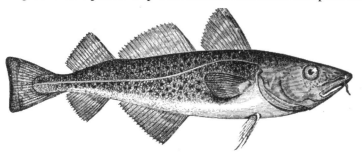

Hook-n-Line Ling Cod

with Steamed Shellfish, Creamy Mashed Potatoes, Grilled Zucchini and Roasted Garlic

1 cup fish stock	Salt and pepper
8 Manila steamer clams	2 (7-ounce) ling cod filets
6 mussels	Creamy Mashed Potatoes (recipe follows)
6 tablespoons butter	Grilled Zucchini (recipe follows)
2 teaspoons minced chives	Roasted Garlic (recipe follows)
2 tablespoons olive oil	Chopped tomato for garnish

In a medium pot, bring fish stock to a boil over medium-high heat. Add clams and mussels, cover, and steam until shells open. Discard any unopened clams or mussels. Remove clams and mussels with a slotted spoon and keep warm. Strain broth and return to pot. Reduce broth by half. Remove from heat and whisk in the butter and chives until butter is melted.

In a large skillet, heat olive oil over medium heat. Season ling cod with salt and pepper. Place fish in hot pan and cook for 3 to 4 minutes. Turn fish over and cook an additional 4 minutes or until fish is cooked through but still moist in the center.

To serve, divide mashed potatoes onto two plates. Place grilled zucchini around the potatoes. Place clams and mussels around potatoes. Pour sauce over potatoes. Place ling cod on top of potatoes. Garnish with roasted garlic cloves and chopped tomatoes. Serves 2.

Creamy Mashed Potatoes

2 russet potatoes, peeled and quartered
3 tablespoons butter
1/4 cup heavy cream

Cook potatoes in boiling salted water until tender. Drain well. Mash with butter and cream until smooth. Set aside and keep warm.

Grilled Zucchini

1 zucchini, cut lengthwise into strips
Olive oil
Salt and pepper

Brush zucchini strips with olive oil then season with salt and pepper. Grill or broil until tender, about 3 minutes.

Roasted Garlic

12 cloves garlic, peeled
1/2 cup olive oil
1/4 cup fresh orange juice

Preheat oven to 350 degrees.

Place garlic, olive oil, and orange juice in a small oven-proof sauce pan. Bring to a boil on the stove, then cover and place in the oven for 10 to 15 minutes or until very tender. Set aside.

John Newman, Chef
Sunset West Restaurant

Pan Fried Oregon River Trout

Oregon is a trout fisherman's paradise! Many of the local streams are well kept secrets of the avid fly fisherman in search of rainbow, brook and German browns. Cook the fresh fish within a few hours of catching them.

6 fresh trout, cleaned and washed
1 cup flour
1 cup finely chopped hazelnuts
Salt and white pepper to taste

2 eggs
1 tablespoon water
1 cup vegetable oil
Lemon slices

Mix flour, hazelnuts, salt, and white pepper together in a shallow dish. In a separate shallow dish, whisk together eggs and water. Dredge trout in flour mixture. Dip into egg mixture, then dredge again in flour mixture. Heat oil in a cast iron skillet over medium-high heat. Fry the trout about 4 minutes on each side, or until golden brown. Serve with lemon slices. Serves 6.

Alfred Popp

 # *Seafood Burrito*

1 tablespoon oil
1/2 cup diced bell peppers
1/2 cup diced onion
1 cup prepared salsa
1 cup diced tomatoes
1/2 cup chopped fresh cilantro
1/2 cup chopped black olives
1/2 cup fresh orange juice

1 pound fish, such as red snapper,
    cut into 1-inch cubes
4 flour tortillas
4 ounces pepper jack OR Monterey Jack
    cheese, shredded
1/2 cup chopped green onions
Sour cream

In a large skillet, heat oil over medium heat. Sauté bell peppers and onion until soft. Add salsa, tomatoes, cilantro, olives, and orange juice and simmer until liquid has reduced and mixture is thick. Add fish and simmer, stirring often, until fish is cooked through. Heat tortilla in another skillet and place on plate. Place 1/4 of fish mixture in the center of tortilla and sprinkle with 1/4 of the cheese and 1/4 of the green onions. Roll up and garnish with the sour cream. Repeat until all of the ingredients are used. Enjoy. Serves 4.

Cosmos Cafe

Sea Otters

Sea otters once lived around the rim of the Pacific Ocean from Baja California to Japan. Between their discovery in 1741 and their protection in 1911, sea otters were hunted nearly to extinction for their beautiful thick pelts.

Otters have made a remarkable recovery in the last 80 years. Once thought extinct, the California population is spreading slowly up and down the coast. A few sea otters from Alaska have been reintroduced off the Washington coast.

From a distance, its hard to tell a resting sea otter from a floating log, at least until it moves. And sea otters never stay still for long. They dive for food or roll over and over in the water, cleaning their thick fur.

You won't see wild sea otters in Oregon—the last one was killed north of Newport around 1906. In the early 1970s, scientists released Alaskan sea otters off Cape Arago and Port Orford on the southern Oregon coast. By 1980, though, the colonies had died out.

Sea otters are the smallest marine mammals and, like whales and seals, they're warm blooded, breathe air and nurse their young. Although not as completely adapted to living in the open sea as other marine mammals, they're well-suited to life along the coast.

Sea otters live in shallow water near shore. Their eyesight is good above and below the surface, and they also use their keen sense of touch to help find food. When they're not diving for shellfish, otters spend their time grooming or resting at the surface or on a beach.

Sea otters usually use their strong jaws and flat molars to crack open shellfish. If a shell's too tough for that, an otter puts a rock on its chest, holds the shell with its paws and pounds it on the rock until the shell breaks.

Sea otters have a pocket under each foreleg formed by a fold of loose skin. When diving, they store urchins and crabs they've already caught in the pocket and keep looking for more.

Otters groom constantly, rubbing and "chewing" their fur to keep it clean and water-resistant. They blow into it to maintain the layer of air which keeps the cold seawater away from their skin.

To maintain their body temperature in the cold water, sea otters eat about 25% of their weight in shellfish protein each day. Otters scoop abalone from the shell with their lower canine teeth and crush crabs with their molars.

At the surface, sea otters often swim on their backs, paddling with one webbed hind foot and then the other. While diving for food, otters swim on their stomachs, flexing their bodies up and down like a porpoise.

Small but sensitive, sea otter's front paws are essential to their way of life. Otters find food by touch under rocks and in murky water. They use their paws to crack open shellfish and to groom their thick fur.

Like harbor seals, sea otters sometimes come ashore to rest on rocky beaches, but they're just as likely to sleep at sea. They float on their backs, often wrapped in kelp to keep from drifting away.

Branzino in Aceto

This is one of the classic all time favorite fish dishes from the Genoa restaurant. Filets of red snapper are marinated in a spicy mixture of anchovy, garlic, olive oil, and mustard, then dredged in flour and fried. Serve with lemon.

1 (2-ounce) can anchovies
2 tablespoons chopped fresh parsley
1 tablespoon dry mustard
2 cloves garlic, chopped
3/4 teaspoon dry oregano
1/2 teaspoon black pepper
1/3 cup extra virgin olive oil
1/4 cup lemon juice

2-1/2 pounds red snapper filets,
    all bones removed
Flour
Salt and pepper
3 eggs, lightly beaten
Olive oil for cooking
Lemon wedges

Combine anchovies, parsley, mustard, garlic, oregano, 1/2 teaspoon pepper, and 2 tablespoons of the olive oil in the bowl of a food processor. Pulse until almost smooth. With the motor running, add the remaining olive oil in a thin stream until mixture is thick. Stir in lemon juice. Place mixture in a shallow baking dish and marinate the fish in the refrigerator for at least three hours, turning fish occasionally.

Season flour with salt and pepper and place in a shallow dish. Put eggs in another shallow dish. Remove fish from marinade and dredge in flour. Dip in eggs, then dredge in the flour again.

In a large skillet, heat the olive oil over medium-high heat. Fry fish until richly colored on both sides and tender on the inside. Serve with lemon wedges. Serves 8.

Catherine Whims
Genoa

 Grilled Ahi Tuna in Dijon Sauce

1 tablespoon extra virgin olive oil
1 shallot, finely minced
1 cup dry Riesling OR Chardonnay
1 cup heavy cream

2 tablespoon Dijon mustard
2 pounds fresh ahi tuna steaks
1 teaspoon chopped parsley
1 teaspoon coarsely ground pink peppercorns

Heat olive oil in a medium saucepan over medium heat. Add shallot and sauté until translucent. Add wine and simmer until reduced by half. Whisk in cream and Dijon and simmer for about 3 minutes.

Grill or broil tuna steaks until medium-rare, about 4 minutes per side. Place on a serving platter and nap with sauce. Sprinkle with parsley and pink peppercorns. Serve with jasmine rice. Serves 4.

Christophe at Face Rock

Court Bouillon Poached Cod
with Saffron and Julienned Carrots and Leeks

2 quarts water	5 whole black peppercorns
1 lemon, sliced	1 pound cod filets
2 slices onion	2 carrots, julienned
1 teaspoon minced garlic	1 leek (white and pale green part only),
1 teaspoon salt	julienned
2 bay leaves	1/4 teaspoon saffron threads

To make the court bouillon, place water, lemon, onion, garlic, salt, bay leaves, and peppercorns in a straight-sided skillet and bring to a boil. Reduce heat to low and simmer for 15 minutes. Strain court bouillon and discard the solids. Return broth to skillet and return to a simmer over medium-low heat.

Place cod in the simmering court bouillon and simmer for 5 minutes. Add the julienned carrots, leeks, and saffron and simmer an additional 2 to 3 minutes or until the cod is cooked through.

Remove cod and place on a heated serving platter. Skim out the carrots, leeks, and saffron and put on top of the cod. Serves 4.

Colin Cox
Oregon Electric Station Restaurant
and Lounge

Ginger and Shoyu Halibut

This is an easy way to enjoy the fresh halibut season. It is quick and has a high taste factor. Shoyu is a mild Japanese soy sauce and can be found at Asian grocery stores and many supermarkets. The addition of a generous amount of fresh ginger makes a tangy marinade. Serve with a dry Gewurztraminer or Pinot Blanc.

1/4 cup shoyu sauce	1 tablespoon sugar
1/4 cup water	4 1-inch thick halibut steaks
3 tablespoons rice wine vinegar	
2 tablespoons grated fresh ginger,	
grate over bowl to save the ginger juice	

In a shallow glass dish, whisk together shoyu, water, rice wine vinegar, ginger and reserved ginger juice, and sugar. Place halibut steaks in marinade and refrigerate 1 hour, turning once to coat other side.

Preheat broiler. Oil broiling pan and preheat, this is to sear the fish as you begin the cooking process. Place halibut on the broiling pan and place under the broiler, leaving door ajar. Broil 4 minutes on one side. Turn the fish, brush with marinade, and broil an additional 4 minutes. Remove from oven and serve immediately. Serves 4.

Vickki Wettle
Amity Vineyards

Seals and Sea Lions

Seals on the seashore

Watch for what look like piles of gray, five-foot-long slugs at the mouths of bays or atop rocks along the coast. Those are probably harbor seals, hauled out for a nap in the sun. Shy on land, they'll scoot back into the water if you get too close.

Once in the water, curiosity wins out over a harbor seal's shyness. The seals often float upright, only their sleek heads out of water, looking around with big brown eyes. Curiosity satisfied, the seals sink down without a sound.

Sea lions are easy to spot

California sea lions are hard to ignore when they're hauled out of the water, barking on offshore rocks, jetties or floats. They're brown when dry, black when wet. All sea lions have short ears. The males have thick necks and domed foreheads.

Cruising around bays, sea lions paddle slowly with head and back just above water. These playful mammals often body surf on the waves or leap out of water while swimming at high speed.

Seal pups are well cared for

Harbor seals live along the Oregon coast all year long. Large groups gather at nursery sites during May and June when their pups are born. The pups, which can swim almost immediately, nurse on their mother's fat-rich milk for four to six weeks.

Seal pups resting on the beach alone may be waiting for their mothers to return from feeding or they may no longer be nursing. Either way, don't try to help them. Harbor seals have survived on their own for centuries.

Big males move north

Once the summer breeding season is over, male California sea lions migrate north. From late August through early June you can find them in bays, river mouths and on offshore rocks along the Oregon coast. The females and pups stay behind in warmer waters to the south.

Male sea lions are social animals and often gather in groups. Sometimes they float together in a bay, each holding a flipper out of the water to control body temperature. Other times the sea lions gather on buoys or rocks where they bark loud and long.

What is a pinniped?

Pinnipeds, whose name means feather- or fin-footed, are marine mammals with long, paddle-like feet and streamlined, torpedo-shaped bodies. Though pinnipeds spend much of their time in the sea, many rest, molt and give birth on land.

Pinnipeds include the walrus, eared seals and true seals. Eared seals, like sea lions and fur seals, have small ears and rotate their hind limbs forward to walk on land. True seals, like elephant and harbor seals, have no external ears and scoot around on their bellies on land.

Eating

Harbor seals and sea lions eat various fish like smelt, herring and perch, as well as squid and octopus. They eat larger fish at the surface, snapping them into bite-sized pieces, but under water they swallow smaller fish whole.

Staying warm

Humans, seals, and sea lions have similar body temperatures. Although humans must wear special gear to stay warm in the cold sea, seals and sea lions are well insulated with blubber. This layer of fat covered with thick skin and fur keeps icy cold out and body heat in.

Diving

Seals and sea lions are designed for diving. When they begin a dive, their heart rates slow and blood circulates to only the critical organs like the heart and brain. Since their muscles use stored oxygen, they can hold their breath longer.

Swimming

Harbor seals hold their front flippers tightly at their sides, speeding through the water with alternate strokes of their webbed hind feet. Sea lions pull themselves through the water with their paddle-like flippers and use their rear end as a rudder.

Walking

Harbor seals are clumsy on land, humping along on their bellies. Sea lions are more at home on land. They tuck their hind feet under, rise up on their large front flippers and walk on all-fours.

Kalamata Olive Crusted Fish
with Mascarpone Mashed Potatoes

1-1/2 cups finely chopped pitted Kalamata
    olives
1 cup semolina flour
Salt and pepper

4 thick cod filets
2 tablespoons olive oil
Mascarpone Mashed Potatoes
    (recipe follows)

In a small bowl, mix olives and flour together with a fork until well blended. Season filets with salt and pepper. Press olive mixture onto one side of the filets.

Heat olive oil in a large non-stick skillet over medium heat. Place cod filets olive side down in the hot pan. Cook for 10 to 15 minutes or until fish is cooked through and olive crust is firm and crisp on the outside but not burned. Serve over Mascarpone Mashed Potatoes. A delicious side dish would be kale sautéed with shallots and pinenuts. Serves 4.

Mascarpone Mashed Potatoes

4 to 5 russet potatoes
1 cup mascarpone cheese
1 teaspoon thyme

Salt and pepper to taste
Olive oil for drizzling

Peel and quarter potatoes. Cook until tender in boiling salted water. Drain well. Mash until smooth. Add mascarpone and thyme and mash again until smooth and well blended. Season with salt and pepper and drizzle with olive oil.

Kay Kusy-Eliasson

 # Uyak Baked Halibut

1 cup white wine
1 teaspoon salt
1 pound halibut filets
1/2 cup fine cracker crumbs

1 cup mayonnaise
1/2 cup sour cream
1/4 cup chopped green onions
Paprika

Whisk together the wine and salt in a shallow dish. Add the halibut, cover with plastic wrap, and marinate in the refrigerator for 2 hours, turning once.

Preheat oven to 500 degrees. Lightly oil a shallow baking dish.

Remove halibut from marinade and lightly coat in cracker crumbs. Place in prepared baking dish. Mix mayonnaise, sour cream and green onions and spread evenly over halibut. Sprinkle remaining crumbs on top. Bake for about 15 minutes, or until halibut flakes easily. Sprinkle with paprika before serving. Serves 2.

Alan and Alice Beardsley

Puff Pastry

with Oregon Rockfish, Lemon Cream Sauce and Caviar

5 ounces Oregon rockfish filets
1 bunch fresh spinach
1/4 cup cream cheese
1 teaspoon minced garlic
Salt and pepper to taste

1 egg
2 tablespoons water
4 (5-inch) squares frozen puff pastry, thawed
Lemon Cream Sauce (recipe follows)
Caviar

In a medium skillet, add 2 inches of water and bring to a simmer over medium heat. Add rockfish and poach for about 3 minutes. Remove from liquid and set aside to cool.

Wash spinach well then pat dry. Chop coarsely and put into a medium bowl. Chop cool fish and add to spinach. Add cream cheese, garlic, salt, and pepper and mix well.

In a small bowl, whisk egg and 2 tablespoons water until smooth to make the egg wash.

Place 2 squares of puff pastry on a floured board and brush with egg wash. Divide the rockfish mixture in half and place in the center of pastry. Top with the remaining squares of pastry and seal the edges. Brush top of pastries with egg wash.

Preheat oven to 350 degrees.

Place filled pastries on a baking sheet and bake for about 20 minutes, or until golden brown. Divide the Lemon Cream Sauce onto 2 plates. Top with a pastry and garnish with caviar. Serves 2.

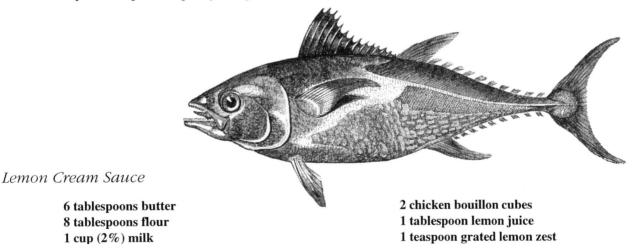

Lemon Cream Sauce

6 tablespoons butter
8 tablespoons flour
1 cup (2%) milk

2 chicken bouillon cubes
1 tablespoon lemon juice
1 teaspoon grated lemon zest

Prepare a roux by melting the butter in a small saucepan over medium heat. Whisk in flour and cook, stirring often, for about 3 minutes.

In a medium saucepan, simmer milk and chicken bouillon cubes together over medium heat. Whisk until bouillon has dissolved. Whisk some of the hot milk mixture into the roux, then pour back into the milk mixture. Cook, whisking constantly, until mixture thickens. Whisk in lemon and lemon zest and heat through.

Brenda Friedich, Chef
Augustines

Barbequed Teriyaki Tuna

3/4 cup purchased teriyaki sauce
2 tablespoons soy sauce
2 tablespoons Chinese black bean sauce

2 large cloves garlic, minced
2 pounds tuna filets

In a large zip-lock plastic bag, combine teriyaki sauce, soy sauce, Chinese black bean sauce, and garlic. Add tuna and seal bag. Marinate 1 hour, turning once.

Prepare barbeque and place a piece of aluminum foil on the center of the grill. Remove tuna from marinade and reserve marinade to brush on tuna while cooking. Place tuna on foil. Cover barbeque and cook until done, about 20 to 30 minutes. Brush with marinade several times while cooking. Serve with rice. Serves 6.

Dorothy Maynard

 # Rum Baked Fish
with Hot Mango Salsa

2 tablespoons peppercorns
10 whole allspice berries
10 whole cloves
1 cup dark rum
1 cup soy sauce

3/4 cup sugar
6 catfish filets OR other firm white fish,
    boneless and skinless
Hot Mango Salsa (recipe follows)

Preheat oven to 425 degrees.

In a medium saucepan, over medium-high heat, toast the peppercorns, allspice and cloves just until spices start to pop. Place spices in a mortar and pestle and crush. Return spices to saucepan and add rum, soy sauce and sugar. Reduce heat to medium and simmer until mixture is reduced by half. Take care that rum does not ignite, cover with a lid if it does.

Strain mixture and discard the spices. Pour liquid into a baking dish and place filets in dish. Marinate 10 minutes. Turn fish and place in oven. Bake for about 10 minutes, or until fish is cooked through. Serve with Hot Mango Salsa. Serves 6.

Hot Mango Salsa

2 ripe mangoes, peeled, and diced
1 red bell pepper, seeded and diced
2 habanero chiles, seeded and minced

3 tablespoons cider vinegar
1/2 teaspoon salt

In a medium bowl, combine all ingredients and mix well. Allow to stand 30 minutes before serving to allow flavors to marry.

Leslie J. W. Mansfield

Seviche

1-1/2 pounds very fresh firm white fish filets,
    such as red snapper, cabazon or ling cod,
    cut into 1/2-inch cubes
1 cup diced red onions
1 cup diced Roma tomatoes
3/4 cup lime juice
1/2 cup chopped cilantro
1/2 cup chopped Italian parsley
1/4 cup lemon juice

1/4 cup olive oil
1 tablespoon minced garlic
1 tablespoon chopped fresh mint
2 teaspoons freshly ground black pepper
1 teaspoon ground coriander
1/2 teaspoon minced jalapeño chile
1/2 teaspoon cumin
1/2 teaspoon minced lime zest
1/2 teaspoon salt

Combine all ingredients in a large bowl and mix well. Cover and refrigerate at least 4 hours or overnight. Serve with rye bread and a chilled dry Gewurztraminer. Serves 6.

Richard Mansfield

Sweetwater's Grilled Grouper
in Banana Leaves with Tropical Papaya-Mango Salsa

Grouper is found throughout the Bahamas and the Florida Keys. The flesh of the fish is tender and sweet, although a little difficult to grill (the banana leaves in this recipe remedy this situation). If you can find grouper fresh, buy it and cook it. This dish is not only delicious, but makes a truly elegant presentation. The banana leaves impart a subtle flavor during cooking and our spicy-sweet and sour Tropical Papaya-Mango Salsa is a perfect accompaniment for the fish.

2 tablespoons fresh Key lime juice OR
    regular lime juice
4 cloves garlic, minced
Salt and freshly cracked pepper to taste

4 (6 to 8-ounce) fresh grouper filets
2 banana leaves*
Tropical Papaya-Mango Salsa (recipe follows)
Lime wedges

In a small bowl, whisk together lime juice, garlic, salt, and pepper. Transfer mixture to a large zip-lock plastic bag. Add grouper and close bag. Marinate for 5 minutes. Remove filets and discard marinade. Using a pair of kitchen shears, cut the banana leaves in half. Wrap the banana leaf around the filet (like an envelope) and secure with wooden toothpicks. Repeat process with remaining filets and banana leaves.

Place the banana leaf packets, toothpick-side up on the grill over medium heat. Cook about 8 to 10 minutes per side or until opaque and flaky, yet still moist. Do not overcook.

Serve the grouper in banana leaves with Tropical Papaya-Mango Salsa and lime wedges to garnish. Fried ripe plantain slices make a nice accompaniment. Serves 4.

    If fresh banana leaves are unavailable, frozen leaves can be found at almost any Asian market.

Tropical Papaya-Mango Salsa

Sweetwater's Caribbean-inspired salsa features the Scotch bonnet chile. Be careful here, this chile is a real dynamo! If you're not a true chilehead, we suggest using only half the chile. The exotic spiciness of the Scotch bonnet chile and the tangy sweetness of the Ruby papaya combine to create a perfect accompaniment for a variety of fresh grilled seafoods.

1 large red onion, diced
1 red bell pepper, diced
1 English cucumber, peeled and diced
1 ripe mango, peeled and diced
1/4 ripe Ruby papaya*; peeled, seeded and
    diced
2 jalapeño chiles, seeded and minced

1 Scotch bonnet chile OR habanero chile, minced
1/2 bunch fresh basil, finely chopped
2 sprigs fresh mint, minced
1/4 cup lime juice
2 tablespoons white wine vinegar
1 tablespoon sugar
Salt and freshly cracked pepper to taste

Combine all ingredients in a large bowl and mix thoroughly. Cover and chill at least 1 hour before serving to allow flavors to marry. Salsa will keep in the refrigerator for up to 3 days.

    Ruby papayas can be found at Latin markets and several supermarkets.

Susan Zimmerman
Sweetwater's Jam House

Pesca Spada Al Forno
(Baked Swordfish with Sicilian Salsa)

1-1/2 pounds swordfish
1 medium onion, thinly sliced
2 cloves garlic, chopped
1/2 cup fresh mint leaves, chopped
1 tablespoon dried oregano
1 tablespoon rosemary

Salt and pepper to taste
1 tablespoon butter
1/4 cup olive oil
1 cup dry white wine
Salsa A Parte (recipe follows)

Preheat oven to 375 degrees. Lightly oil a baking dish just large enough to hold the fish.

Place swordfish in prepared baking dish. Scatter onion and garlic over fish. Top with mint, oregano, and rosemary. Season with salt and pepper. Dot with butter and pour olive oil over. Bake for 10 minutes then pour in the wine. Continue baking until swordfish is cooked through but still moist inside. Serve with Salsa A Parte. Serves 4.

Salsa A Parte

3 tablespoons red wine vinegar
1/2 teaspoon sugar
1/4 cup olive oil
2 tablespoons lemon juice
2 tablespoons mixed chopped fresh herbs,
    such as mint, rosemary and thyme

1 tablespoon chopped fresh parsley
1 tablespoon dried oregano
1 clove garlic, minced
1 tablespoon capers, rinsed
Salt and pepper to taste

In a small bowl, whisk together vinegar and sugar until sugar dissolves. Whisk in the olive oil, lemon juice, fresh herbs, parsley, oregano, and garlic. Stir in capers. Season with salt and pepper.

Patricia Wied, Chef
Nature's Fresh Northwest

Driftwood comes from land and sea

Driftwood floats offshore, waiting for its chance to hit the beach. Currents carry the wood up and down the coast, but once caught by the power of waves, even the largest logs are eventually thrown high up on the sand.

Most driftwood is washed into coastal rivers by storms, floods or erosion. Tree trunks, branches, and logging debris can float out to sea with the rivers and ride the waves back to shore. Packing crates and exotic woods lost at sea can also become driftwood.

Grilled Tuna
with Corn and Cilantro Vinaigrette

3 tablespoons olive oil
2 tablespoons mixed chopped fresh herbs,
    such as basil, chervil, chives, parsley,
    and thyme

2 tablespoons lemon juice
Salt and pepper to taste
6 tuna steaks
Corn and Cilantro Vinaigrette (recipe follows)

In a shallow dish, whisk together olive oil, herbs, lemon juice, salt, and pepper. Place tuna in mixture and marinate 1 hour. Grill tuna over hot coals, brushing with marinade, about 3 minutes per side, or until cooked through but still moist inside. Serve with Corn and Cilantro Vinaigrette. Serves 6.

Corn and Cilantro Vinaigrette

1 small clove garlic, minced
1 teaspoon Dijon mustard
Salt and pepper to taste
1 tablespoon lime juice
1 tablespoon red wine vinegar

1 jalapeño chile, seeded and minced
1/3 cup olive oil
1/2 cup corn kernels
1/4 cup minced fresh cilantro

In a medium mixing bowl, combine garlic, mustard, salt, and pepper and mash with a fork to make a smooth paste. Whisk in the lime juice, vinegar, and minced chile. Whisk in the oil in a thin stream. Stir in corn and cilantro.

Victor Chamorro. Executive Chef
Nature's Fresh Northwest

Taking the best of
both worlds

Where the seafloor is soft and sandy, most animals live either over it or in it. Animals over the sand take advantage of food suspended in the water. Animals buried in it find protection and stability.

Safely anchored in the sand, sea pens, burrowing anemones and sand dollars filter fine bits of food from the water. When predators threaten, anemones and sea pens retract into the sand. When storm waves scour the bottom, sand dollars, too, dig in.

Seared Sea Bass
with Blackberry Oil and Green Peppercorns

1 cup blackberries
1 cup plus 1 tablespoon olive oil
1 tablespoon minced garlic
1 teaspoon lemon juice

Salt and pepper to taste
2 pounds sea bass, cut into 8-ounce pieces
2 tablespoons green peppercorns in brine, minced

In a medium saucepan, combine blackberries, 1 cup olive oil, garlic, lemon juice, salt, and pepper and bring to a boil. Reduce heat to medium-low and simmer for 5 minutes. Strain through a sieve and discard solids. Set aside blackberry oil.

In a large non-stick skillet, heat 1 tablespoon olive oil over medium-high heat. Sear sea bass about 3 minutes per side, or until cooked through but still moist inside.

Divide blackberry oil onto 4 plates. Top with a piece of sea bass. Sprinkle minced green peppercorns over sea bass. Serves 4.

Victor Chamorro, Executive Chef
Nature's Fresh Northwest

Tidal Channels

Tidal channels make ideal nurseries. The gentle currents won't sweep little animals away and the water is too shallow for large predators. There's plenty of food to grow on, too, from tiny algae to shrimps and worms.

Topsmelt (Atherinops affinis)

Known for their bright "racing stripe," topsmelt form large schools in spring, then enter river mouths and estuaries by the hundreds to spawn over the soft mudflats. They attach clusters of BB-sized eggs to strands of eelgrass.

Whale Ballen

Triangular plates called baleen hang from a baleen whale's upper jaw. Made of material much like your fingernails, the overlapping plates are straight on the outside and fringed on the inside where they form a mesh to trap the whale's tiny food.

Nesting Seabirds

Seabirds take refuge in sanctuaries

Nesting seabirds are highly sensitive to disturbances. Hikers, boats or planes that come too close to a colony can panic the adults. They may stampede, leaving nests unguarded, or they may accidentally knock their eggs or chicks into the sea.

To protect seabird nesting colonies, the U.S. Fish and Wildlife Service has designated almost all Oregon coast rocks, reefs and islands as part of the National Wildlife Refuge System. You can't visit the colonies but you can get a good look at some of them from shore.

Seabirds find safety in numbers

During the breeding season, seabirds gather in dense colonies on coastal islands, rocks and cliffs. Thousands of birds of several species may nest in one location. The large number of birds in a colony helps defend the eggs and chicks against predators.

The various seabird species build nests on different sites, though, so there's room for all. Cormorants build bulky nests on rocky cliffs and ledges. Puffins and auklets dig burrows in sandy soil and common murres lay eggs directly on barren rock. Pigeon guillemots nest in rocky cracks and crevices.

Where can we look at nesting birds?

Seabirds nest on coastal rocks, islands and cliffs from April to August. There are large colonies at Haystack Rock in Cannon Beach, Yaquina Head near Newport and Harris Beach north of Brookings. Don't forget your binoculars since the nesting colonies are for the birds only.

Why are murre eggs shaped like pears?

Common murres lay their eggs directly on rocks and ledges without building a nest. Some scientists think the eggs are pear-shaped so that, if bumped, they'll pivot around their narrow end and stay on the ledge rather than roll off to smash on the rocks below.

Seabird Aviary

OREGON COAST
AQUARIUM

Just off Oregon's shores live birds that spend their lives at sea, except for their annual breeding season in summer. Along the shore live other birds that feast on clams, crabs and mussels. An open-air, walk-through aviary at the Oregon Coast Aquarium allows visitors the rare opportunity to see some of these species up close. The aviary is the largest of its kind in North America.

Two pools provide the birds with ample swimming and diving opportunities. A 30-foot rocky cliff rises above the north pool, with ledges and walkways that allow the bird to rest, groom and dive from the cliff face. An underwater viewing window is located at this pool, too, so that visitors can watch the underwater swimming skills for which some of these species are known.

The Aquarium rehabilitates injured and sick seabirds, in a cooperative program with the Oregon Department of Fish and Wildlife.

Seabirds exhibited in the Seabird Aviary include tufted puffins, rhinoceros auklets, pigeon guillemots, common murres and black oystercatchers.

Shellfish

OREGON COAST
AQUARIUM

Steamed Crab with Ponzu Sauce

4 live Dungeness crabs

Ponzu Sauce (recipe follows)

Place a steamer basket or rack in a large pot. Add enough water to come 3 inches up the sides. Cover pot and bring water to a boil over high heat. Lift lid and using tongs to avoid burning yourself, place crabs on rack. Steam about 10 minutes per pound. Crab is done when shell changes to bright orange. Remove the top shell, or carapace, and discard the feathery gills. Crack open the body and legs and extract the meat. Serve with Ponzu Sauce for dipping. Serves 4.

Ponzu Sauce

1/2 cup Japanese soy sauce
1/4 cup lemon juice

1/4 cup rice wine vinegar
2 green onions, chopped

Combine all ingredients and pour into dishes for dipping.

Yash Terakura
Daruma Japanese Restaurant

Crab and Shrimp Casserole

2 cups cooked rice
1 cup mayonnaise
1 cup tomato juice
1/2 cup minced onion
1/4 cup minced green bell pepper

1/4 cup milk
1/2 pound crab meat
1/2 pound bay shrimp
Salt and pepper to taste
Slivered almonds

Preheat oven to 350 degrees. Oil a 9-inch by 13-inch baking dish.

In a large bowl, combine rice, mayonnaise, tomato juice, onion, bell pepper, and milk and stir to combine. Gently fold in crab and shrimp. Season to taste with salt and pepper. Sprinkle almonds on top. Bake for about 1 hour, or until liquid is absorbed. Serves 6 to 8.

Patty Martin

Scallops in Artichokes

This recipe is very simple and features Oregon wine as well as Oregon seafood.

4 large artichokes
Juice and peel of 1 lemon
2 tablespoons minced onion
2 bottles Pinot Gris

4 tablespoons unsalted butter
2 tablespoons minced ham
1 pound large sea scallops

Wipe the artichokes with the lemon juice to prevent browning. Cut off the bottom so the artichokes can sit upright. Trim the leaves evenly. Place upright in a pot large enough to hold them. Add lemon peel and minced onion. Pour in 1 bottle of Pinot Gris. Cover tightly and bring to a boil. Reduce heat to medium-low and steam for about 1 hour, or until artichokes are very tender and most of the liquid has evaporated.

Remove artichokes and carefully hollow out the middle down to the heart. Discard the choke.

If there is much cooking liquid remaining in the pot, reduce until almost dry. Take care not to burn. Discard lemon peel. Add butter to the pot and melt over medium heat. Add the ham and sauté 1 minute. Add scallops and sauté until just cooked through. Stuff the artichokes with the scallops and drizzle cooking liquid over. Serve with remaining bottle of Pinot Gris and crusty bread. Serves 4.

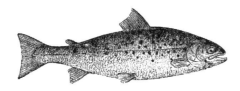

Wendy J. Kreutner
Autumn Wind Vineyards

Steamed Mussels in Wine

4 cups water
2 cups dry white wine
1/2 cup minced parsley
4 green onions, chopped
3 lemon slices
1 clove garlic, minced

1 sprig fresh rosemary
1/8 teaspoon pepper
4 to 5 pounds mussels, scrubbed and
  debearded
1/2 cup melted butter
Juice of 1 lemon

In a large pot, combine water, wine, parsley, green onions, lemon slices, garlic, rosemary, and pepper and bring to a boil over high heat. Add the mussels and cover pot. Cook, stirring once or twice, about 5 to 8 minutes, or until mussels open. Discard any unopened mussels.

Stir together melted butter and lemon juice and pour into dishes for dipping. Serve mussels with slotted spoon. Serve with lots of crusty bread. Serves 6.

Chris Pontrelli and Jim Burly

Chilled Kamilche Mussels
with Citrus Salsa

24 Kamilche mussels, scrubbed and debearded
2 cups dry white wine

Ice
Citrus Salsa (recipe follows)

Place mussels in a large pot with a tight fitting lid. Pour in wine and cover tightly. Bring to a boil then reduce heat to medium-low and steam until the mussels open, about 5 minutes. Discard any unopened mussels. Place cooked mussels and ice in a strainer over the sink to cool.

Place drained mussels, still in their shells, on a large plate. Pour Citrus Salsa into the shells and chill for 1 hour before serving. Serves 4.

Citrus Salsa

1 green bell pepper, finely chopped
1 red bell pepper, finely chopped
1 yellow bell pepper, finely chopped
1 small red onion, finely chopped
1 jalapeño chile, minced

3 tablespoons minced fresh cilantro
Juice of 2 oranges
Juice of 2 lemons
Juice of 2 limes

Combine all salsa ingredients in a medium bowl and let stand for 1 hour to allow flavors to marry.

Brenda Fredrick
Augustines Restaurant

Beaches get annual face-lifts

Winter waves drag sand off the beaches and deposit it in bars just offshore. That leaves only coarse grains and pebbles on the narrow steep beaches. But spring waves are gentler. They push the sandbars back toward shore, rebuilding the wide beaches of summer.

Each winter, heavy storm waves batter the coastline. This annual assault slowly erodes the headlands and wears down the cliffs. There's little cliff-top homeowners can do but watch as their yards are eaten away by waves.

Jetties and headlands catch the drift

As each wave hits the beach, it carries sand grains a short distance. The angle of the wave determines which direction the sand grains drift—usually north in winter, south in summer. In Oregon, these motions cancel each other out, leaving the beaches with no net drift.

Jetties interrupt the movement of sand along the shore at the mouths of rivers and bays. Gradually the sand builds up, forming broad beaches. Sandy beaches also form where rocky headlands block the flow of sand.

Dungeness Crab Cakes
with Sun-dried Tomato Remoulade

2 tablespoons olive oil
1 yellow onion, finely diced
1 Bermuda onion, finely diced
1 yellow bell pepper, finely diced
1 poblano chile, finely diced
2 pounds crab meat
1-3/4 cups fresh bread crumbs
1/2 cup heavy cream

2 eggs, separated
1-1/2 teaspoons white pepper
3/4 teaspoon kosher salt
1/4 teaspoon Tabasco sauce
Flour
1/2 cup peanut oil
Sun-dried Tomato Remoulade (recipe follows)

Heat olive oil in a large skillet over medium heat. Add the yellow onion, Bermuda onion, bell pepper, and poblano chile and sauté until translucent. Remove to a sieve and allow excess liquid to drained off and let mixture cool completely.

Place onion mixture in a large bowl and add crab meat, bread crumbs, egg yolks, white pepper, salt, Tabasco sauce and mix gently and evenly, taking care not to break up crab meat too much.

Place egg whites in a shallow bowl and whisk until lightly beaten. Place flour in another shallow dish. Add peanut oil to a large skillet and heat over medium heat. Form crab mixture into balls the size of a golf ball and flatten into disks. Dip in egg whites, allow the excess to drip off, then dip in flour. Fry about 2 minutes per side. Repeat until all crab mixture is used. Serve with Sun-dried Tomato Remoulade. Serves 8.

Sun-dried Tomato Remoulade

1 stalk celery, finely minced
1/4 cup finely minced red or green bell pepper
1/4 cup finely minced green onion
3 tablespoons finely minced oil-packed
    sun-dried tomatoes
2 tablespoons finely minced Bermuda
    onion

2 tablespoons finely minced parsley
1-1/4 cups mayonnaise
3/4 cup Creole mustard OR whole-grain
    mustard
2 tablespoons paprika
3/4 teaspoon cayenne pepper
1/4 teaspoon white pepper

In a large bowl, combine all ingredients and blend well. Chill 1 hour before serving to allow flavors to marry.

Matthew Lasof, Executive Chef
Avalon Grill and Cafe

Common Murre (Uria aalga)

Common murres (a type of seabird) are uncommonly good divers. Propelled by sturdy wings, the murres move swiftly under water in pursuit of schooling fish. They've been known to dive as deep as 240 feet and to stay under as long as 72 seconds.

!!!Oysters Ellen!!!

I made up this recipe for my wife, Ellen, since it contains many of her favorite flavors. She likes very spicy, hot food, so I advise reducing the amount of chile flakes if you would like a milder version.

1 tablespoon olive oil
1 pint fresh Yaquina Bay oysters, drained
1/2 cup minced green onions

3 thick slices bacon, minced
2 teaspoons dried red hot chile flakes
2 tablespoons lemon juice

Preheat oven to 450 degrees.

Put olive oil in a shallow oven-proof baking dish just large enough to hold the oysters. Put in the oysters in a single layer. Sprinkle the green onions, bacon, and chile flakes over the oysters. Then sprinkle over the lemon juice. Bake for about 12 to 15 minutes, or until cooked through. Serves 4.

Pete Wall

 Dominic's Hangtown Fry

8 slices bacon
1/2 cup diced green pepper
5 eggs
2 tablespoons water

1/4 teaspoon salt
1/2 cup cracker crumbs
12 medium oysters, drained

In a large non-stick skillet, fry the bacon until crisp over medium heat. Remove bacon and crumble onto a paper towel to drain. Add green pepper to the skillet and sauté until just tender. Remove green pepper with a slotted spoon and drain on a paper towel. Remove all but 1/4 cup of the bacon drippings and discard.

In a medium bowl, beat the eggs, water and salt together. Place the cracker crumbs in a shallow dish. Dip the oysters in the egg mixture then dredge in the crumbs. Return the skillet with the reserved 1/4 cup bacon drippings to medium heat. Quickly brown the oysters on both sides. Top the oysters with the bacon and green pepper. Pour the remaining egg mixture over the oysters. Reduce heat to medium-low and cook, without stirring, until eggs are firm and the bottom is lightly browned. Slide out of the skillet onto a hot platter and serve at once. Serves 4.

Dominic Dulcick
Pacific Sea Food Company

 *Deviled Oysters*

2 tablespoons olive oil
1/4 cup minced onion
1 quart oysters and their liquor
1/2 cup finely chopped celery
2 tablespoons minced parsley

2 tablespoons ketchup
2 tablespoons lemon juice
2 tablespoons Worcestershire sauce
1/4 teaspoon Tabasco sauce
1 cup cracker crumbs

Preheat oven to 425 degrees. Lightly butter a shallow baking dish.

In a large skillet, heat the olive oil over medium heat. Add the onion and sauté until lightly browned. Add the oysters and their liquor and simmer until their edges curl. Remove skillet from heat and remove oysters with a slotted spoon

and put in a large bowl. Add celery, parsley, ketchup, lemon juice, Worcestershire sauce, and Tabasco sauce to the skillet and whisk to blend. Stir in cracker crumbs. Add crumb mixture to the oysters and toss gently. Turn mixture into the prepared baking dish. Bake for about 10 to 15 minutes or until the oysters are sizzling hot. Serves 6.

Dominic Dulcick
Pacific Sea Food Company

 Lemon Lager Manila Steamer Clams

2 tablespoons butter
1 tomato, diced
1/2 cup chopped leek (white and pale green
    parts only)
2 cloves garlic, minced

1/2 teaspoon minced fresh basil
1/2 teaspoon minced fresh oregano
1-1/2 pounds Manila steamer clams
1 (6-ounce) bottle Saxer Lemon Lager beer

Melt butter in a large pot over medium heat. Add tomato, leeks, garlic, basil, and oregano and sauté until fragrant, about 3 minutes. Add steamer calms and toss with the mixture. Add Saxer Lemon Lager and cover pot tightly. Cook until clams open. Discard any unopened clams. Serve in a deep bowl with garlic bread and drawn butter. Serves 2.

Gary Stevenson, Chef
Wayfarer Restaurant

Rugged Oregon Coast
Dungeness Crab Cakes
with Lemon and Garlic Aioli

4 ounces fresh sole, chilled
1 bunch fresh chives, chopped
1/4 cup crushed ice
Salt and pepper to taste

1/2 cup heavy cream
8 ounces fresh Dungeness crab meat
2 tablespoons olive oil
Lemon and Garlic Aioli (recipe follows)

Place the sole, chives, ice, salt, and pepper in the bowl of a food processor. Pulse together while slowly adding the cream until all is incorporated. Mixture should have a smooth texture.

Place fish mixture in a large bowl and fold in the crab meat, taking care not to overmix. Divide mixture into 6 portions and shape into patties. Heat olive oil in a large skillet over medium heat. Sauté crab cakes until golden brown on both sides. Serve topped with Lemon and Garlic Aioli. Rice pilaf and a fresh vegetable make a nice accompaniment. Serves 2.

Lemon and Garlic Aioli

1 egg yolk
1 tablespoon lemon juice
1/2 teaspoon minced garlic
1/2 cup olive oil

1 tablespoon chilled fish stock OR chicken
    stock
Salt and pepper to taste.

In a medium bowl, combine egg yolk, lemon juice and garlic and whisk until blended. Slowly drizzle in half of the olive oil, whisking vigorously. When mixture starts to resemble mayonnaise, whisk in the fish stock. Then continue to slowly pour in the remaining olive oil while whisking vigorously. Season with salt and pepper.

John Newman, Chef
Sunset West Restaurant

Leopard Shark (Triakis semifasciata)

Black-spotted leopard sharks don't look much like the man-eating monsters of page and screen. These shy sharks have small mouths on the underside of their heads for nipping-off clam siphons and sucking worms from the sand.

Red Rock Crab (Cancer productus)

A male red rock crab carries his mate for several days until she molts her hard shell and he can fertilize the eggs. He stays with the female until her new shell is hard enough to protect her. She carries the eggs under her belly until they hatch into drifting plankton.

Baked Oysters

1 pint oysters
Cracker crumbs

2 eggs, beaten
2 tablespoons milk

Preheat oven to 500 degrees. Lightly oil an 8-inch by 8-inch baking dish.

Dip the oysters in the cracker crumbs and place in prepared baking dish. Mix eggs and milk together and pour over oysters. Bake for 10 minutes, or until oysters are cooked and eggs are set. Serves 2.

Joyce Hall

Diving Seabirds

Now you see them now you don't

Beyond the waves breaking on shore, diving seabirds float on the ocean. Suddenly one arches its body and disappears under the water. The bird pops up again several yards away, having captured a seafood supper. Diving seabirds are physically fit for life at sea and many come ashore only to nest. They have muscular legs set far back on their heavy bodies, just under the tail. These birds are excellent underwater swimmers but awkward when walking on land.

Eating

Most diving seabirds are fish-eaters. Some dive after open sea schooling fish like smelt and herring while others swim to the bottom for sole, sculpins and blennies. Almost all seabirds supplement their diet with squid or shrimp from time to time.

Kicking

Many seabirds have webbed feet like ducks. When the foot pushes back against the water, the web spreads out to make the most of the downstroke. When the foot moves forward, the web folds together again to reduce drag.

Swimming

Some diving birds use their wings under water as well as in the air. Blunt wings flapping, these birds seem to fly through the sea. Their feet trail behind like rudders helping them steer.

Keeping warm

Seabirds depend on their feathers to protect them from the cold ocean. A seabird's dense plumage keeps a layer of warm air next to its skin. Seabirds maintain their feathers with oil from a preen gland at the base of their tail.

Seeing

To you, everything looks blurry underwater, but not to diving ducks. Some have eyelids like contact lenses that correct their vision. Others focus their eyes by flexing special muscles to change the shape of the lens.

Yaquina Bay Oyster Bake

Breading Mixture

1/2 cup fine bread crumbs   1 tablespoon onion powder
1/2 cup cracker meal   1 teaspoon dill
1/2 cup corn meal

Place breading mixture in a shallow bowl. Stir together with a fork.

1 pound shucked small oysters
1/2 cup lemon juice
Salt and pepper to taste

Preheat oven to 400 degrees. Oil a 9-inch by 13-inch baking dish with vegetable spray.

Dip oysters in lemon juice then dredge in breading mixture. Place in prepared baking dish and season with salt and pepper. Bake for 10 minutes, turn oysters over and bake an additional 10 minutes. Serve with purchased tartar sauce. Serves 4.

Elaine Stark

Vermilion Rockfish (Sebastes miniatus)

You may know this vermilion fish as red snapper at the market or as rockcod on the end of a fishing line. It's not really a snapper or a cod, though, but one of the many species of rockfish. In their juvenile stage, they lack the bright red coloring of adults. Instead they sport brownish, mottled hues which assist them in hiding among the blades in the kelp forest canopy.

Sablefish (Anoplopoma fimbria)

The torpedo-shaped sablefish is also known as black cod. Most don't migrate long distances, but they do move from shallow water in summer to deeper water in winter. Sablefish make up one of Oregon's major deep water longline fisheries.

Lingcod (Ophiodon elongatus)

Lingcod lie on the bottom scanning the water with their keen eyes. They lunge after bite-sized fish that swim by, eating almost any species that will fit into their gaping jaws.

Seafood Mama Crab Cakes
with Flame-Roasted Red Pepper Cream Sauce

1 egg
2 tablespoons lemon juice
2 teaspoons Dijon mustard
1/8 teaspoon Tabasco sauce
Salt and freshly cracked pepper to taste
1 pound fresh Dungeness crab meat

3/4 cup Japanese panko bread crumbs
3 green onions, finely chopped
2 tablespoons olive oil
Flame-Roasted Red Pepper Cream Sauce
  (recipe follows)
Lemon slices and chopped parsley for garnish

In a large bowl, whisk together egg, lemon juice, Dijon mustard, and Tabasco sauce, salt, and pepper until well blended. Add Dungeness crab meat, panko bread crumbs, and green onions and fold together until blended but not over mixed. Divide mixture into 6 portions and shape into patties.

In a large skillet, heat olive oil over medium heat. Add crab cakes and sauté until golden on both sides. Serve on Red Pepper Cream Sauce and garnish with lemon slices and chopped parsley. Serve with one of Oregon's crisp dry Rieslings. Serves 2.

Flame-Roasted Red Pepper Cream Sauce

4 red bell peppers
1/2 cup dry white wine
1/2 teaspoon minced garlic

1/2 teaspoon minced shallots
2 tablespoons heavy cream
Salt and pepper to taste

Cut peppers in half and remove seeds and veins. Place on a hot barbeque or over a gas burner and roast until blackened all over. Remove from barbeque and immediately place in plastic bag. Let cool for 15 minutes. Remove and discard skins. Place peppers, wine, garlic, and shallots in the bowl of a food processor and puree. Pour mixture through a sieve, pressing on the solids, into a small sauce pan. Add the cream and season with salt and pepper. Simmer over medium-low heat until slightly thickened, stirring often to avoid scorching.

Jack Koberstein, Chef
Seafood Mama

 # Crab Maryland

3 tablespoons butter
2 tablespoons flour
1 cup half and half
3 hard cooked eggs, sieved

1 teaspoon minced chives
1 pound crab meat
1/4 cup dry sherry

In the top of a double-boiler, melt the butter over medium heat. Whisk in the flour until well blended. Pour in the half and half slowly, whisking constantly. Cook until mixture is thick, while continuing to whisk. Stir in hard cooked eggs and chives. Stir in crab and sherry and heat through. Serve in pastry cups or over rice.

Patty Martin

Sweetwater's Pepper Prawns

In Jamaica, these fiery hot prawns are sold by the side of the road. We make a similar version that are served cold with our own Caribbean-style cocktail sauce and fresh limes. We recommend several ice-cold beers as an excellent accompaniment.

8 to 10 Scotch Bonnet chiles OR habaneros
1/3 cup salt
2-1/2 pounds tiger prawns

Sweetwater's Caribe Cocktail Sauce
   (recipe follows)
Lime wedges

Place chiles in the bowl of a food processor and pulse until smooth. Place chile puree, salt, and prawns in a nonreactive bowl and toss well. Let stand for 15 minutes.

Heat a large skillet over medium-high heat. Add prawns and sauté until all the prawns are firm and turn bright pink. Remove prawns from heat and chill. Serve with Sweetwater's Caribe Cocktail Sauce, lime wedges, and an ice-cold beer to quench the fire.

Sweetwater's Caribe Cocktail Sauce

1 small Bermuda onion, finely chopped
1 clove garlic, minced
1 cup tomato ketchup
1/4 cup Key Lime juice OR regular lime juice
1 tablespoon extra hot horseradish

1 teaspoon amber rum
1/2 teaspoon cayenne pepper
1/2 teaspoon chili powder
1/8 teaspoon paprika

Combine all ingredients and blend well. Chill before serving. Sweetwater's Caribe Cocktail Sauce will keep several weeks in the refrigerator.

Susan Zimmerman
Sweetwater's Jam House

Restaurant Index

Amity Vineyards
18150 Amity Vineyards Road S.E.
Amity, OR 97101
503-835-6451

Augustines
19706 Highway 18
McMinnville, OR 97128
503-843-3225

Autumn Wind Vineyard
15225 N.E. North Valley Road
Newberg, OR 97132
503-538-6931

Avalon Grill and Cafe
4630 S.W. Macadam Avenue
Portland, OR 97201
503-227-4630

Bay House
5911 S.W. Highway 101
Lincoln City, OR 97367
541-996-3222

Bethel Heights Vineyard, Inc.
6060 Bethel Heights Road N.W.
Salem, OR 97304
503-378-0565

Bugatti's Ristorante
18740 Willamette Drive
West Linn, OR 97068
503-636-9555

Chez Claudine French-American Restaurant
1220 W. Central
Coquille, OR 97423
541-396-5312

Chez Jeanette
7150 Old Highway 101
Gleneden Beach, OR 97388
541-764-3434

Christophe at Face Rock
3225 Beach Loop Drive
Bandon by the Sea, OR 97411
541-347-3261

Cosmos Cafe
740 W. Olive Street
Newport, OR 97365
541-265-7511

Dan and Louis Oyster Bar Restaurant
208 S.W. Ankeny
Portland, OR 97205
503-227-5906

Daruma Japanese Restaurant
8860 S.W. Hall Boulevard
Beaverton, OR 97223
503-526-0129

Digger O'Dell's Oyster Bar and Restaurant
532 S.E. Grand Avenue
Portland, OR 97214
503-238-6996

Elizabeth's Cafe
3135 N.E. Broadway
Portland, OR 97232
503-281-8337

Flying Gull Restaurant
1143 Chetco Avenue
Brookings, OR 97415
541-469-2173

Genoa
2832 Southeast Belmont Street
Portland, OR 97214
503-238-1464

Gracie's At Smuggler's Cove
333 S.E. Bay Boulevard
Newport, OR 97365
541-265-2523

Greenleaf Restaurant
49 N. Main
Ashland, OR 97250
541-482-2808

Hotel Newport
3019 North Coast Highway
Newport, OR 97365
541-265-9411

Il Piatto Restaurant
2348 S.E. Ankeny
Portland, OR 97214
503-236-4997

Jake's Famous Crayfish Restaurant
401 S.W. 12th Avenue
Portland, OR 97205
503-220-1859

Kah Nee Ta Resort
Warm Springs, OR 97761
1-800-554-4786 or 541-232-1112

Kearnville Steak and Seafood Restaurant
186 Siletz Highway
Lincoln City, OR 97367
541-994-6200

Mo's® Enterprises, Inc
622 S.W. Bay Boulevard
Newport, OR 97365
541-265-7512

Nature's Fresh Northwest
8024 E. Mill Plain Boulevard
Vancouver, WA 98664
360-695-8878

Oregon Electric Station Restaurant and Lounge
27 East 5th Avenue
Eugene, OR 97401
541-485-4444

Pacific Fish and Oyster Company
3380 Powell Boulevard
Portland, OR 97202
503-223-4891

The Sea Basket
Boat Basin Drive
Charleston, OR 97420
541-888-5711

Sea Hag Restaurant and Lounge, Inc.
Post Office Box 278
Depoe Bay, OR 97341
541-765-2760

Seafood Mama
721 N.W. 21st Avenue
Portland, OR 97209
503-222-4121

Siletz Tribal Smokehouse
272 S.E. Highway 101
Depoe Bay, OR 97341
541-765-2286 or 1-800-828-4269

Spadas "Bistro" at Gold Beach
1020 S. Ellensburg
Gold Beach, OR 97444
541-247-7732

Sunset West Restaurant
33200 Cape Kiwanda Drive
Pacific City, OR 97135
541-965-6789

Sweetwater's Jam House
1017 S.E. 33rd Avenue
Portland, OR 97214

Trout House Restaurant
Post Office Box 4355
Sunriver, OR 97707
541-593-8880

Tualitan Vineyards
10850 N.W. Seavey Road
Forest Grove, OR 97116
503-357-5005

Umpqua Brewing Company
328 S.E. Jackson
Roseburg, OR 97470
541-672-0452

University of Oregon
Faculty Club
Collier House
1170 East 13th Street
Eugene, OR 97403
541-346-5268

Wayfarer Restaurant
Oceanfront and Gower Street
Cannon Beach, OR 97110
541-436-1180

Western Culinary Institute
1316 S.W. 13th Avenue
Portland, OR 97201
503-223-2245

Winterborne Fine Dining From the Sea
3520 N.E. 42nd
Portland, OR 97213
503-249-8486

Index

Ahi Tuna
  Black Sesame Seed Crusted Ahi ... 96
  Grilled Ahi Tuna in Dijon Sauce ... 102
Appetizers and Salads
  Asian Dungeness Crab Cakes ... 19
  Clam and Cheese Dip ... 16
  Coconut Beer Battered Prawns ... 21
  Cozze Ripini (Stuffed Mussels on the Half Shell) ... 15
  Crab and Artichoke Dip ... 22
  Crab Salad ... 18
  Hot Crab and Jalapeno Dip ... 20
  Hot Crab Dip ... 15
  Mo's Oyster Night Bean and Shrimp Salad ... 19
  Savory Smoked Salmon and Sausage Pie ... 23
  Seafood Slaw ... 18
  Smoked Salmon Log ... 16
  Smoked Salmon Pate ... 17
  Smoky Salmon Spread ... 16
  Tillamook Toast ... 20
Asian Dungeness Crab Cakes ... 19

Baked Oysters ... 126
Baked Swordfish with Sicilian Salsa (Pesca Spada Al Forno) ... 111
Barbequed Teriyaki Tuna ... 108
Beans
  Mo's Oyster Night Bean and Shrimp Salad ... 19
Billi Bi Soup ... 32
Black Sesame Seed Crusted Ahi ... 96
Bouillabaisse ... 33
Bouillabaisse a la Kernville ... 30
Branzino in Aceto ... 102
Brodetto Di Portorecanti ... 41
Broiled Salmon Steaks ... 71
Broiled Salmon Steaks with Dill Butter ... 84
Broiled Salmon Steaks with Hazelnut Frangelico Butter ... 73
Broiled Thresher Shark with Chilean Sauce ... 93

Cabazon
  Cabazon with Crawfish and Chipotle Salsa ... 97
Cabazon with Crawfish and Chipotle Salsa ... 97
Calamari (squid)
  Cioppino D'Oro ... 59
Catfish
  Rum Baked Fish with Hot Mango Salsa ... 108
Chilled Kamilche Mussels with Citrus Salsa ... 121
Cioppino ... 39
Cioppino D'Oro ... 59
Clam and Cheese Dip ... 16
Clams
  Bouillabaisse a la Kernville ... 30
  Brodetto Di Portorecanti ... 41
  Cioppino ... 39
  Cioppino D'Oro ... 59
  Clam and Cheese Dip ... 16
  Lemon Lager Manila Steamer Clams ... 124
  Linguini and Clams a la Yachats ... 49
  Pacific Seafood Chowder ... 32
  Paella ... 51
  Sea Hag Bouillabaisse ... 37
  Sea Hag Clam Chowder ... 38
  Seafood Gumbo ... 35
Coastal Salmon Medallions ... 72
Coconut Beer Battered Prawns ... 21
Cod
  Brodetto Di Portorecanti ... 41
  Court Bouillon Poached Cod ... 103
  Kalamata Olive Crusted Fish ... 106
  Trout House Fishermans Stew ... 31
Cool Salmon Steaks and Vegetables ... 83
Court Bouillon Poached Cod ... 103
Cozze Ripini (Stuffed Mussels on the Half Shell) ... 15

Crab
  Asian Dungeness Crab Cakes ... 19
  Bouillabaisse ... 33
  Bouillabaisse a la Kernville ... 30
  Cioppino ... 39
  Coastal Salmon Medallions ... 72
  Crab and Artichoke Dip ... 22
  Crab and Shrimp Casserole ... 119
  Crab Maryland ... 128
  Crab Salad ... 18

Dungeness Crab Cakes ... 122
Granchio (Crab Cappelini) ... 47
Hot Crab and Jalapeno Dip ... 20
Hot Crab Dip ... 15
Linguini and Clams a la Yachats ... 49
Papa's Cioppino ... 36
Rugged Oregon Coast Dungeness Crab Cakes ... 125
Sea Hag Bouillabaisse ... 37
Seafood Mama Crab Cakes ... 128
Seafood Pasta ... 47
Steamed Crab with Ponzu Sauce ... 119
Tillamook Toast ... 20
Trout House Fishermans Stew ... 31
Crab and Artichoke Dip ... 22
Crab and Shrimp Casserole ... 119
Crab Maryland ... 128
Crab Salad ... 18
Crawfish
Cioppino ... 39

"Dan & Louis Oyster Bar" Oyster Stew ... 33
Deviled Oysters ... 124
Dominic's Hangtown Fry ... 123
Dungeness Crab Cakes ... 122

Fettucine with Mussels ... 54
Fish Stock ... 29

Ginger and Shoyu Halibut ... 103
Granchio (Crab Cappelini) ... 47
Grilled Ahi Tuna in Dijon Sauce ... 102
Grilled Salmon with Salsa Piccante ... 68
Grilled Tuna with Corn and Cilantro Vinaigrette ... 112
Grouper
Sweetwater's Grilled Grouper ... 110

Halibut
Bouillabaisse ... 33
Bouillabaisse a la Kernville ... 30
Brodetto Di Portorecanti ... 41
Cioppino D'Oro ... 59
Ginger and Shoyu Halibut ... 103
Halibut with Beurre Blanc Sauce ... 92
Pacific Seafood Chowder ... 32
Sea Hag Bouillabaisse ... 37
Uyak Baked Halibut ... 106
Halibut with Beurre Blanc Sauce ... 92
Hook-n-Line Ling Cod ... 99
Hot Crab and Jalapeno Dip ... 20
Hot Crab Dip ... 15

Kalamata Olive Crusted Fish ... 106

Lemon Lager Manila Steamer Clams ... 124
Ling Cod
Hook-n-Line Ling Cod ... 99
Linguine Alla Pescatora ... 61
Linguini and Clams a la Yachats ... 49
Lobster
Brodetto Di Portorecanti ... 41

Mo's Oyster Night Bean and Shrimp Salad ... 19
Mo's Oyster Stew ... 35
Mo's Seafood Cioppino ... 29
Monkfish
Oven Baked Marinated Monkfish ... 91
Moules Au Saffron ... 56
Mussels
Billi Bi Soup ... 32
Brodetto Di Portorecanti ... 41
Chilled Kamilche Mussels with Citrus Salsa ... 121
Cioppino ... 39
Cioppino D'Oro ... 59

Cozze Ripini (Stuffed Mussels on the Half Shell) ... 15
Fettucine with Mussels ... 54
Moules Au Saffron ... 56
Mussels Marsala ... 56
Pacific Seafood Chowder ... 32
Seafood Saffron Risotto ... 50
Steamed Mussels in Wine ... 120
Mussels Marsala ... 56

Oven Baked Marinated Monkfish ... 91
Oyster and Corn Chowder ... 40
Oysters
"Dan & Louis Oyster Bar" Oyster Stew ... 33
Baked Oysters ... 126
Bouillabaisse a la Kernville ... 30
Deviled Oysters ... 124
Dominic's Hangtown Fry ... 123
Mo's Oyster Stew ... 35
Mo's Seafood Cioppino ... 29
Oyster and Corn Chowder ... 40
Oysters Ellen ... 123
Pacific Seafood Chowder ... 32
Yaquina Bay Oyster Bake ... 127
Oysters Ellen ... 123

Pacific Seafood Chowder ... 32
Paella ... 51
Pan Fried Oregon River Trout ... 100
Pan Seared Chinook Salmon with Hazelnut Crust ... 82
Pan Seared Salmon with Eggplant, Tomatoes and Garlic ... 81
Papa's Cioppino ... 36
Pasta
Fettucine with Mussels ... 54
Granchio (Crab Cappelini) ... 47
Linguini and Clams a la Yachats ... 49
Moules Au Saffron ... 56
Mussels Marsala ... 56
Rigatoni Garibaldi ... 54
Rock Shrimp and Riesling ... 49
Scallops in Wine Sauce ... 58
Seafood Pasta ... 47

Pasta and Rice
Cioppino D'Oro ... 59
Fettucine with Mussels ... 54
Granchio (Crab Cappelini) ... 47
Linguine Alla Pescatora ... 61
Linguine and Clams a la Yachats ... 49
Moules Au Saffron ... 56
Mussels Marsala ... 56
Paella ... 51
Rigatoni Garibaldi ... 54
Rock Shrimp and Riesling ... 49
Rock Shrimp and Scallop Risotto ... 55
Scallops in Wine Sauce ... 58
Seafood Pasta ... 47
Seafood Saffron Risotto ... 50
Yellow Eye Rock Fish ... 60
Pesca Spada Al Forno (Baked Swordfish with Sicilian Salsa) ... 111
Pesto Crusted Salmon ... 79
Prawns
Bouillabaisse ... 33
Bouillabaisse a la Kernville ... 30
Brodetto Di Portorecanti ... 41
Cioppino ... 39
Cioppino D'Oro ... 59
Coconut Beer Battered Prawns ... 21
Scallops in Artichokes ... 120
Sea Hag Bouillabaisse ... 37
Sweetwater's Pepper Prawns ... 129
Trout House Fishermans Stew ... 31
Puff Pastry with Oregon Rockfish ... 107

Red snapper
Branzino in Aceto ... 102
Brodetto Di Portorecanti ... 41
Red Snapper with Goat Cheese and Peppercorns ... 98
Seafood Burrito ... 100
Snapper Vera Cruz ... 93
Red Snapper with Goat Cheese and Peppercorns ... 98
Rice
Paella ... 51
Rock Shrimp and Scallop Risotto ... 55
Seafood Saffron Risotto ... 50
Rigatoni Garibaldi ... 54
Risotto
Rock Shrimp and Scallop Risotto ... 55
Seafood Saffron Risotto ... 50

Rock Fish
  Yellow Eye Rock Fish ... 60
Rock shrimp
  Brodetto Di Portorecanti ... 41
  Linguine Alla Pescatora ... 61
  Paella ... 51
  Rock Shrimp and Riesling ... 49
  Seafood Saffron Risotto ... 50
Rock Shrimp and Riesling ... 49
Rock Shrimp and Scallop Risotto ... 55
Rockfish
  Papa's Cioppino ... 36
  Puff Pastry with Oregon Rockfish ... 107
Rugged Oregon Coast Dungeness Crab Cakes ... 125
Rum Baked Fish with Hot Mango Salsa ... 108

Salads
  Crab Salad ... 18
  Mo's Oyster Night Bean and Shrimp Salad ... 19
  Seafood Slaw ... 18
Salmon
  Bouillabaisse ... 33
  Brodetto Di Portorecanti ... 41
  Broiled Salmon Steaks ... 71
  Broiled Salmon Steaks with Dill Butter ... 84
  Broiled Salmon Steaks with Hazelnut Frangelico Butter
    ... 73
  Cioppino ... 39
  Cioppino D'Oro ... 59
  Coastal Salmon Medallions ... 72
  Cool Salmon Steaks and Vegetables ... 83
  Grilled Salmon with Salsa Piccante ... 68
  Mo's Seafood Cioppino ... 29
  Pacific Seafood Chowder ... 32
  Pan Seared Chinook Salmon with Hazelnut Crust ... 82
  Pan Seared Salmon with Eggplant, Tomatoes and Garlic
    ... 81
  Pesto Crusted Salmon ... 79
  Salmon A La Baltimore ... 78
  Salmon and Shrimp Cakes ... 67
  Salmon Chowder ... 30
  Salmon Loaf ... 81
  Salmon Sauté with Shiitake Mushrooms ... 69
  Salmon Scampi ... 78
  Salmon Steaks Teriyaki ... 71
  Salmon with a Spicy Honey-Lavender Glaze ... 85
  Salmone En Agrodolce ... 69

  Salt Grilled Chinook Salmon ... 70
  Sea Hag Bouillabaisse ... 37
  Seafood Gumbo ... 35
  Seafood Pasta ... 47
  Smoked Salmon Log ... 16
  Smoky Salmon Spread ... 16
  Steamed Salmon in Nori ... 70
Salmon A La Baltimore ... 78
Salmon and Shrimp Cakes ... 67
Salmon Chowder ... 30
Salmon Loaf ... 81
Salmon Sauté with Shiitake Mushrooms ... 69
Salmon Scampi ... 78
Salmon Steaks Teriyaki ... 71
Salmon with a Spicy Honey-Lavender Glaze ... 85
Salmone En Agrodolce ... 69
Salsa
  Baked Swordfish with Sicilian Salsa ... 111
  Rum Baked Fish with Hot Mango Salsa ... 108
  Tropical Papaya-Mango Salsa ... 110
Salt Grilled Chinook Salmon ... 70
Savory Smoked Salmon and Sausage Pie ... 23
Scallops
  Bouillabaisse ... 33
  Bouillabaisse a la Kernville ... 30
  Cioppino ... 39
  Cioppino D'Oro ... 59
  Rock Shrimp and Scallop Risotto ... 55
  Scallops in Wine Sauce ... 58
  Sea Hag Bouillabaisse ... 37
  Seafood Gumbo ... 35
  Trout House Fishermans Stew ... 31
Scallops in Artichokes ... 120
Scallops in Wine Sauce ... 58
Sea bass
  Brodetto Di Portorecanti ... 41
  Seared Sea Bass ... 113
Sea Hag Bouillabaisse ... 37
Sea Hag Clam Chowder ... 38
Seafood
  Baked Swordfish with Sicilian Salsa ... 111
  Barbequed Teriyaki Tuna ... 108
  Black Sesame Seed Crusted Ahi ... 96
  Branzino in Aceto ... 102
  Broiled Thresher Shark with Chilean Sauce ... 93
  Cabazon with Crawfish and Chipotle Salsa ... 97
  Court Bouillon Poached Cod ... 103
  Ginger and Shoyu Halibut ... 103
  Grilled Ahi Tuna in Dijon Sauce ... 102
  Grilled Tuna with Corn and Cilantro Vinaigrette ... 112

Halibut with Beurre Blanc Sauce ... 92
Hook-n-Line Ling Cod ... 99
Kalamata Olive Crusted Fish ... 106
Oven Baked Marinated Monkfish ... 91
Pan Fried Oregon River Trout ... 100
Puff Pastry with Oregon Rockfish ... 107
Red Snapper with Goat Cheese and Peppercorns ... 98
Rum Baked Fish with Hot Mango Salsa ... 108
Seafood Burrito ... 100
Seafood Gumbo ... 35
Seared Sea Bass ... 113
Seviche ... 109
Snapper Vera Cruz ... 93
Sweetwater's Grilled Grouper ... 110
Uyak Baked Halibut ... 106
Yellowfin Tuna with Blackberry Vinaigrette ... 98
Seafood Burrito ... 100
Seafood Gumbo ... 35
Seafood Mama Crab Cakes ... 128
Seafood Pasta ... 47
Seafood Saffron Risotto ... 50
Seafood Slaw ... 18
Seared Sea Bass ... 113
Seviche ... 109
Shark
Brodetto Di Portorecanti ... 41
Shellfish
Baked Oysters ... 126
Chilled Kamilche Mussels with Citrus Salsa ... 121
Crab and Shrimp Casserole ... 119
Crab Maryland ... 128
Deviled Oysters ... 124
Dominic's Hangtown Fry ... 123
Dungeness Crab Cakes ... 122
Lemon Lager Manila Steamer Clams ... 124
Mo's Seafood Cioppino ... 29
Oysters Ellen ... 123
Rugged Oregon Coast Dungeness Crab Cakes ... 125
Scallops in Artichokes ... 120
Seafood Mama Crab Cakes ... 128
Steamed Crab with Ponzu Sauce ... 119
Steamed Mussels in Wine ... 120
Sweetwater's Pepper Prawns ... 129
Yaquina Bay Oyster Bake ... 127
Shrimp
Bouillabaisse ... 33
Cioppino ... 39
Cioppino D'Oro ... 59
Crab and Shrimp Casserole ... 119
Mo's Oyster Night Bean and Shrimp Salad ... 19

Paella ... 51
Papa's Cioppino ... 36
Rigatoni Garibaldi ... 54
Salmon and Shrimp Cakes ... 67
Sea Hag Bouillabaisse ... 37
Seafood Gumbo ... 35
Seafood Pasta ... 47
Seafood Saffron Risotto ... 50
Seafood Slaw ... 18
Trout House Fishermans Stew ... 31
Skate
Seafood Gumbo ... 35
Smoked Salmon
Savory Smoked Salmon and Sausage Pie ... 23
Smoked Salmon Pate ... 17
Smoked Salmon Log ... 16
Smoked Salmon Pate ... 17
Smoky Salmon Spread ... 16
Snapper Vera Cruz ... 93
Sole
Rugged Oregon Coast Dungeness Crab Cakes ... 125
Soups and Stews
"Dan & Louis Oyster Bar" Oyster Stew ... 33
Billi Bi Soup ... 32
Bouillabaisse ... 33
Bouillabaisse a la Kernville ... 30
Brodetto Di Portorecanti ... 41
Cioppino ... 39
Fish Stock ... 29
Mo's Oyster Stew ... 35
Mo's Seafood Cioppino ... 29
Oyster and Corn Chowder ... 40
Pacific Seafood Chowder ... 32
Papa's Cioppino ... 36
Salmon Chowder ... 30
Sea Hag Bouillabaisse ... 37
Sea Hag Clam Chowder ... 38
Seafood Gumbo ... 35
Trout House Fishermans Stew ... 31
Squid
Linguine Alla Pescatora ... 61
Papa's Cioppino ... 36
Steamed Crab with Ponzu Sauce ... 119
Steamed Mussels in Wine ... 120
Steamed Salmon Wrapped in Nori ... 70
Sweetwater's Grilled Grouper ... 110
Sweetwater's Pepper Prawns ... 129
Swordfish
Baked Swordfish with Sicilian Salsa ... 111

Index

Thresher Shark
    Broiled Thresher Shark with Chilean Sauce ... 93
Tillamook Toast ... 20
Trout
    Pan Fried Oregon River Trout ... 100
Trout House Fishermans Stew ... 31
Tuna
    Barbequed Teriyaki Tuna ... 108
    Black Sesame Seed Crusted Ahi ... 96
    Grilled Ahi Tuna in Dijon Sauce ... 102
    Grilled Tuna with Corn and Cilantro Vinaigrette ... 112
    Seafood Gumbo ... 35
    Yellowfin Tuna with Blackberry Vinaigrette ... 98

Uyak Baked Halibut ... 106

White fish
    Cioppino ... 39
    Mo's Seafood Cioppino ... 29
    Puff Pastry with Oregon Rockfish ... 107
    Seafood Burrito ... 100
    Seviche ... 109

Yaquina Bay Oyster Bake ... 127
Yellow Eye Rock Fish ... 60
Yellowfin Tuna
    Yellowfin Tuna with Blackberry Vinaigrette ... 98
Yellowfin Tuna with Blackberry Vinaigrette ... 98